When Our Parents Need Us Most

When Our Parents *Need* Us *Most*

Loving Care in the Aging Years

David L. McKenna

Harold Shaw Publishers
Wheaton, Illinois

ISBN 978-0-87788-902-1

Cover design by David LaPlaca

Cover photo © 1994 by Luci Shaw

Library of Congress Cataloging-in-Publication Data

McKenna, David L. (David Loren), 1929-
    When our parents need us most : loving care in the aging years / David L. McKenna.
    p. cm.
  ISBN 978-0-87788-902-1
    1. Aging parents—Care—United States. 2. Aging parents—United States—Family relationships. 3. Spiritual life—Christianity. I. Title.
HQ1064.U5M46 1994
306.874—dc20   93-42150
                                                     CIP

99 98 97 96 95 94

10 9 8 7 6 5 4 3 2 1

Contents

INTRODUCTION   vii

CHAPTER 1   1

Living with the Inevitable: Aging

CHAPTER 2   11

Honoring Old Age: Self-Worth

CHAPTER 3   19

Knowing When to Step Down: Retirement

CHAPTER 4   29

Severing the Symbols: Independence

CHAPTER 5   43

Choosing between Parents: Alienation

CHAPTER 6   49

Recycling the Generations: Heredity

CHAPTER 7   57

Parenting Our Parents: Roles

CHAPTER 8   65

Borrowing on Trust: Finances

CHAPTER 9   73

    Handling Our Emotions: Guilt

CHAPTER 10   81

    Meeting Our Mortality: Sickness

CHAPTER 11   89

    Dealing with Doubt: Salvation

CHAPTER 12   99

    Sightings of Heaven: Death

CHAPTER 13   111

    Learning from Jesus: Caregiving

RIGHTS AND RESPONSIBILITIES OF THE
CHRISTIAN CAREGIVER   123

ENDNOTES   125

Introduction

Jim, Beth, Bob, and Bonnie all asked me the same question at separate times: "What book are you writing now?" Flattered by their interest, I answered, "Tentatively, it's titled *When Our Parents Need Us Most* or *When Our Parents Grow Old.*" Their common response took me by surprise. With just the slightest variation in words, each of them pleaded, "Finish it soon. I need it *now.*"

Jim, the president of a publishing company, in his early fifties, went on to explain that he and his wife were trying to delay the decision to move an eighty-two-year-old mother into a nursing home.

Beth, almost forty and an administrative assistant to a college president, reported being at a loss in trying to counsel her mother, who felt torn between her responsibilities to her husband at home and her own mother, who had fallen and broken her hip in a distant city.

Bob, mid-forties and the vice-president of a theological seminary, told of his thwarted desire to show his love for a non-Christian father whose lung cancer had spread so that the terminal diagnosis had been shortened to a matter of days.

Bonnie, wife of a physician and not yet fifty, said that her husband treated deadly diseases, but none of them compared to the Alzheimer's that had reduced her mother to a zombie four years ago.

Behind these real-life dilemmas is the sobering fact that we are entering an era in which the increasing life span of our parents is creating a crisis of caregiving for adult children. Admittedly, we are not ready for this new level of responsibility with all the changing dynamics of medical breakthroughs, life support systems, nursing homes, living wills, Medicaid, and Medicare. Our readiness to respond is even more limited by the fact that we have not been forced to consider these changes from a biblical point of view. Yet, like Jim, Beth, Bob, and Bonnie, we want to put contemporary meaning to

God's commandment to "Honor your father and mother." *What does it really mean for us, as caregivers, to honor our aging parents in the name of Christ?*

This book is a hindsight search for biblical principles children of aging parents can follow as Christian caregivers. I say *hindsight* because my wife and I have been through multiple crises of care with our four aging parents, two of whom died in their sixties and two of whom lived into their nineties. Although the insights of our experience may be highly personalized and nonprofessional, they are honest expressions of our deepest love and lingering hurt. So, to all sons and daughters of aging parents whose phones will inevitably ring with news of crisis, I invite you to join me in the search for the biblical principles and the Christlike spirit that will qualify us as caregivers who honor our parents and please God.

David L. McKenna

CHAPTER 1

Living with the Inevitable

Aging

Sooner or later, your phone will ring. Ours did—not once or twice, but four times over a brief period of six years. Each time the ring signalled crisis for an aging parent. Are you ready for the ring?

Ring . . . The first call came in 1974 as an airport page in Indianapolis, Indiana: "Dr. David McKenna. Go to the nearest white telephone for an urgent call." My sister wept as she told me that the doctor had just diagnosed leukemia in our sixty-five-year-old mother, who lived alone in Ypsilanti, Michigan. According to the history of such cases, Mom had nine months to live.

R-Ring . . . Two years later, in 1976, a second phone call came with the startling effect of an alarm ringing in the middle of the night. Calling from Sarasota, Florida, to Seattle, Washington, my father's second wife tried to be calm as she reported Dad's heart attack. While waiting for the medics to arrive, he had lost oxygen to the brain. Dad had been reduced to a sixty-nine-year-old vegetable.

1

R-R-Ring . . . Another two years went by before a visiting pastor felt compelled to call us with the fear that my wife's elderly parents could no longer manage their own home in Spring Arbor, Michigan, without the danger of fire or injury. Dad Voorheis, at the age of eighty-eight, showed signs of physical weakening every day, and Mom Voorheis, four years younger, suffered the effects of advancing senility. The pastor recommended a local retirement home with graduated levels of care.

R-R-R-Ring . . . The fourth call came to our home in Seattle barely two years after we had moved Mom and Dad Voorheis into the retirement village. Our family doctor in Spring Arbor called with the news that Dad Voorheis had fallen and broken his back. With the voice of medical authority, he told us that we had no alternative but to put Dad in the nursing home for prolonged care. Mom, who could not understand what was going on, would have an adjoining bed.

Looking back, I can hardly comprehend the complexities with which we had to deal as a family. Distance made it almost impossible for my wife and me to give close personal attention to our parents' problems. Except for regular visits, our care had to be communicated by transcontinental telephone from Seattle to Michigan, to Florida, and back again to Michigan. Our own obligations to family and work deepened our dilemma as distant caregivers. With four children at home, my wife could not give extended periods of time to be with her aging parents. Furthermore, my position as a university president demanded my presence on campus, and, except for the privilege of occasional side trips to Florida to see my father, time and cost limited the visits.

A Tangled Web

Our personal complications, however, were minor when compared with the tangled web of physical, relational, economic, and spiritual difficulties with which we had to deal. The gamut of *physical difficulties* for our parents ran from natural aging and early senility to acute leukemia, a mysterious heart attack, and death to a brainstem.

Then add to that the complexities of *family relationships*. My dad had divorced my mother in 1962 and married again, a decision that shifted his affection, increased the distance from his children, and forced us to make choices between him and Mom. On the other side of the family, the relational problems were different, but still difficult. As the son-in-law of Dad and Mom Voorheis, I had to make decisions about their physical and economic welfare that required unbroken trust. Dad Voorheis never doubted my intentions, but Mom, in one moment of lucidity on the day that I sold the family home, snapped at me from the back seat of the car, "What have you done to me? You've taken away my home and sent me to the poorhouse!" Senility had released the fear and hostility that were buried so deeply in the soul of a saint.

Economic decisions involved more than the sale of the family home or health insurance. Our mom's acute leukemia prompted my sister and me to say to the doctor, "Spare no cost in her care." Then, shortly after her death, Dad's heart attack introduced us to a totally different set of economic decisions. With the brainstem dead and all hope of recovery gone, the cost of intensive hospital care proved to be prohibitive. He had to be moved to a nursing home with the prospect of surviving for months or years in his vegetable state. Who would pay the cost? His second wife? His children? Or how would we share?

No sooner had we resolved these questions about my parents than economic problems of my wife's aging parents caught up with us. When they could no longer keep their own home, it had to be sold. But the limited assets of a lifetime in the parish ministry would not last long. With the prospect of spending the rest of their lives in a nursing home with twenty-four-hour care, how would we cover their costs? Medicaid did not ease their haunting fear of being impoverished and dying in the disgrace of the poorhouse, even if it were a Christian nursing home. Their economic crisis required us to take a crash course in the durable power of attorney, estate gifts to family, and Medicare provisions for the aging.

Underneath all of these complexities, there were *spiritual challenges* that we could not anticipate. I discovered that my mom, as a last hope for her healing from leukemia, had sent ten dollars and a handkerchief to a faith healer on television. What would I say to her? At the other extreme, my dad had denied his faith in Jesus Christ at the time of his divorce. For years he had stonewalled me on spiritual matters. What might I have said to him before his heart attack?

Nor can I forget my wife's sense of guilt for not going immediately to be with her father when a nurse took it upon herself to call us and say that he was dying. Add to that her mother's sudden burst of hostility, coupled with a rejection of the church she loved. What do you say? How do you pray? What do you do? When our parents grow old, there are no simple answers.

Nightmare in the Nineties

The facts are in. On the short swing of one generation, dominant numbers in our population are shifting from teenage youth to senior citizens. Advertising is the giveaway. A generation ago, Madison Avenue lived and died on the code word *young* in its ads. Who can ever forget the "Pepsi Generation"? Today, however, these same ads and commercials feature a middle-aged actress promoting Ultress hair coloring, a grandparent taking a grandchild to McDonald's, a "Golden Girl" pushing a vitamin pill, and a senior golfer selling clubs. Madison Avenue is simply reflecting the facts: America is aging and "gray power" is rising. Our senior citizens are fast becoming the largest and most powerful segment in our society.

As always, we have tried to cushion the impact of aging with euphemistic names and age-defying jokes. Rather than admitting that we are becoming "old," "elderly," or "aged," our preference is to talk about "senior citizens" in the "graying of America." And, of course, none of us wants to admit that we are getting old.

In a sermon taped for *Preaching Today,* Ray Stedman said that he looked into the mirror one morning and said, "What's a young guy like you doing in an old body like this?" His good humor is consistent with the often-told story about parents in their eighties who don't want to go to a retirement village or a nursing home with those "old people." We are not surprised, then, when researchers report that only 53 percent of persons over eighty admit that they are "old," 36 percent consider themselves "middle aged," and 11 percent still think of themselves as "young."[1]

Likewise, with our life expectancy moving from 69.7 years in 1960 to 75.4 years in 1990, distinctions are now being made among those whom we used to lump into the single category of being "old." Persons from the age of sixty-five to seventy-four are now being identified as the "young old," while those between seventy-five and eighty-four are the "middle old," and only those over the age of eighty-five are the "old."[2]

Despite our efforts to rename aging and to joke about becoming old, emerging facts still feed the fear that the "graying of America" will become a "national nightmare." In their book *Parenting Your Aging Parents,* Francine and Robert Moskowitz chose the subtitle *Guidance through the Family Nightmare of the 90s.* Here are some of the facts upon which they base their dire prediction:[3]

- "Old" Americans over the age of eighty-five are the fastest-growing age group in our population, and persons over seventy-five make up the next fastest-growing group.
- Thirty-one million Americans are now over the age of sixty-five. This age group is growing at twice the rate of the general population.
- Seven million older Americans suffer from some form of chronic illness that requires long-term care.

- Twenty-five percent of all Americans over the age of sixty-five (and 50 percent of those over the age of eighty-five) cannot survive a week without outside help, usually from children or relatives.
- One-third to one-half of all working Americans also care for parents or relatives thirty-five or more hours per week.
- One-third of women care for young children and aging parents at the same time.
- Persons over sixty-five commit 25 percent of all suicides even though they are currently only 11 percent of the population.
- By 2000 A.D. persons over sixty-five will account for 20 percent of our total population.
- A majority of all families seeking aid for aging parents have difficulty knowing where to go and how to proceed.

Facts such as these account for the identification of adult children in the next generation as GRUMPIES—Grown Up Mature Professionals. A caricature of their role in an Associated Press cartoon shows them, not only as educated and affluent professionals in their field, but also as children of aging parents who carry in their ever-present briefcase "a checkbook with a small balance, a brochure on saving for college, and *Literature on Retirement Homes for Parents*."[4] In other words, adult children from the 1990s and on will have to plan for the care of aging parents as a standard part of their role and responsibility. Yet, because our attitudes, our policies, or our actions are not ready for this revolution, the care of aging parents may become what the Moskowitzes call "the family nightmare of the 90s."

A Christian's Promise

Let me repeat: sooner or later, your phone will ring. It may be the ring of urgency in the middle of the night that makes you sit straight up in your bed and leaves you sleepless for the rest of the night. Or it may be the ring of a routine call during the day that also takes you by surprise and pushes all other priorities aside. Still again, it may be the ring that you expected at any time, the ring that sets in motion a planned series of responses to cope with the inevitable. Emotionally, however, there is no way to prepare for a situation that you have never known before. The crisis of an aging parent is unique in itself. Even if we have dealt successfully with the crisis of one parent, the next one will be totally different.

No one can explain, for instance, why the aging, crises, and death of a mother are different from that of a father. Perhaps it is a difference in roles or a difference in bonding. Or does the distinction run so deeply in our hearts and souls that only eternity can unravel the mystery? Whatever the reason, ask anyone who has experienced the crises of aging parents. They will tell us the same story. Dad and Mom are different, not in our love for them, but in the legacy they leave us. They mean something different to us, their crises evoke different emotions in us, and their loss leaves a different kind of hole that can never be filled.

While no one can fully anticipate all of the surprises that come with the experience of aging parents, and no one can use their experience to frame twelve steps for successful sons and daughters, we can learn something from each other. We can learn together a biblical perspective on aging that runs counter to the attitudes of our secular culture. We can learn how a lifetime of love translates into a quality of care when our parents grow old. Of course, we can also learn from each other's errors. Some cautions along the way will keep us from stumbling over the same rocks. Best of all, we can learn about the unforeseen blessings that come with advancing age, both for our parents and for us. These "spiritual serendipities" or pleasant surprises may well define the difference between a secular and a Christian view of aging. With eternity in view, a Christian sees in aging the continuity of God's time, the opening of wider horizons, and the giving of new gifts to the child of God. Isn't that the meaning of our creation in the image of God? When our parents grow old, we see them living closer to God, growing taller in grace, and moving faster toward heaven.

Books about children as caregivers for aging parents are flooding the market. Some of the books give "how-to-do-it" details for understanding the processes and coping with the crises of aging parents. *Parenting Our Parents* by Francine and Robert Moskowitz is a good example and a helpful reference. Others are written from a Christian point of view with an autobiographical touch that provides a basis for recommending steps in caring for our parents. Tim Stafford's book *As Our Years Increase* is an invaluable resource from this perspective. My writing complements these books with a different touch and tone. I have intentionally weighted my writing toward our relational struggles as children of parents who share a common faith and yet confront the physical, emotional, social, and spiritual crises that aging inevitably brings. More emphasis, then, is put on the real-life story of my family facing the urgent issues, uncertain choices, and uneasy resolutions of caring for our aging fathers and mothers.

Three specific goals guide my writing. First, I want to flesh out the meaning of God's commandment to "Honor your father and mother" in the contemporary setting of prolonged life with all of its relational complications. *How do we honor, respect, and dignify our parents in the crises of our day?*

Second, I want to communicate the Spirit of Christ, who fulfilled God's commandment to put priority on caring for our parents. He warned us against the attitude of the Pharisees, "But you say that if a man says to his father or mother: 'Whatever help you might otherwise have received from me is Corban' (that is, a gift devoted to God), then you no longer let him do anything for his father or mother. Thus you nullify the word of God by your tradition that you have handed down" (Mark 7:11-13). *How do we make the gift of caring for our parents a spiritual priority in our day?*

Third, I want to pursue the promise of the Lord for those who honor their parents: "that you may live long in the land the LORD your God is giving you" (Exod. 20:12). *How do we claim God's promise of long life in a good land as we care for our fathers and mothers today?* The answer may lie in a simple paraphrase of the Golden Rule: *Do unto your parents as you want your child to do unto you.* If love is the motive that turns the cycle of the generations, the "national nightmare" can become the Christian's promise.

CHAPTER 2

Honoring Old Age
Self-Worth

Secularism is a thief that has robbed our parents of the honor of aging. To be honored as they grow old, our parents need to be valued for their past experience, given our unconditional love, and respected for their continuing contribution. How do you assure your aging parents these gifts of self-worth?

The Thief of Eternal Time

With its worship of the "Radical Now," secularism has robbed our aging people of the honor of time. By definition, secularism is "This Age-ism." Neither the past nor the future has value to a secularist. Everything of honor is squeezed into the present moment of time. But what a price is paid for the loss of the past. The perspective of history, which older people alone can bring to a culture, is gone. A "community of memory," which Robert Bellah finds essential to continuity in a culture, no longer exists.[1] No wonder the youth of today are condemned to repeat the hard lessons that their fathers and mothers learned. No wonder the curriculum in higher education has devalued the history of Western civilization. What good is the past if everything of value and honor can be personally experienced in the present moment of time? At best, the lessons of an older generation are irrelevant; at worst, they are repressive because they restrict the freedom of a younger generation that must experience everything for itself.

Secularists who squeeze time into the "Radical Now" lose the future as well as the past. We see the symptoms of this loss in current attitudes toward children. If the future is in the eyes of the young, the prognosis is poor. From the impulse of pain in the half-formed eyes of an aborted baby to the confusion in the discerning eyes of a child torn between the affections of divorced parents, the future looks bleak. The profile of symptoms could go on and on. Not the least is the evidence that children of single parents, along with elderly people on welfare, constitute the "new poor" among us. All of the facts to support this tragic conclusion are in, but as yet, neither the government nor the church has responded as the "benevolent community" that we claim as our point of pride among the nations of the world.

The loss of a sense of eternity is the greatest loss of all. When time has no past or future in human terms, it certainly cannot have continuity in spiritual terms. To think of time without beginning or end is beyond the comprehension of the secular mind. To think that we are created by an eternal God to live forever in heaven or hell is, to the secular mind, nothing more than a fanciful idea of an outmoded past. Yet this is the concept of time in which the elderly find meaning. As the days of life are shortened, their minds and spirits begin to stretch toward eternity. Whether they lived for good or evil, elderly people find themselves asking the haunting question "Is this all there is?" To answer yes does not satisfy. Eternity is built into our souls, and if we deny our nature we rob ourselves, and especially our older people, of meaning. The anticipation of life after death is absolutely necessary to give old age its value and meaning. Without the anticipation of eternity, there is no hope.

The Thief of Unconditional Love

Secularism has also robbed us of the unconditional love that our parents need when they grow old. To the "Radical Now" the secularist adds an obsession with the "Radical Self." Love becomes as limited as time. No one counts except the all-consuming self. Self-giving, the very essence of Christian character, is ridiculed, except in one circumstance. If self-giving can be traded for something of self-interest, it will be used in the barter. Skeptics even go so far as to say that self-interest is always the motive behind self-giving. Any act of love, they say, can be explained by the benefit received by the giver. Whether it's relief from guilt, the warm feeling of doing good, the obedience to religious convictions, or the duty to another human being, an act of love is nothing more than another expression of self-interest. Of course, such a jaundiced viewpoint rules out the self-sacrifice that Jesus taught and practiced. To think of dying for an enemy, without a return except the risk of rejection, is inconceivable to the secularist. To the Christian, however, "love is an unlimited warranty."

Aging parents become innocent victims of secular self-interest. We are all aware of the changes in culture that have made the extended family—parents, children, and grandparents living together—a rarity. Career mobility, urban housing, living costs, reduced family size, working couples, and day-care programs have all militated against extended families, which include aging parents in the household. Retirement villages and nursing homes are the substitutes. Not that our parents object. There are compensating values in the independence of parents, grandparents, and grandchildren. But with that independence is the danger of losing the assurance of unconditional love and the "hands-on" care that our aging parents need. What was once an obligation for total life-care of parents can be reduced to an economic expectation. Someone else will provide the care if the sons and daughters (or the State) will pay the bills. One of the sentences spoken most often by aging parents to their children may well be, "I don't want to be a burden." The words carry their own pathos.

The Thief of Meaning

Secularism has robbed our aging parents of a third value. With the robbery of time and love goes the theft of meaning. A secularist is a person who seeks meaning in "radical happiness." As we know, happiness depends upon external circumstances, not upon internal quality. *Joy* is the strong biblical word that captures the quality of life that is independent of circumstances. Jesus is our example. In Hebrews we read of Him who "for the joy set before him endured the cross, scorning its shame, and sat down at the right hand of the throne of God" (12:2). To the secularist the "joy of the cross" is an oxymoron. There can be no joy in pain or suffering. Certainly there can be no "Radical Happiness"—a feeling of well-being for the "Radical Self" in the "Radical Now." To seek this end of meaning is to be a materialist, a hedonist, and ultimately a nihilist. Even Henry David Thoreau saw the dead end of such pursuit when he advised, "If you want to be rich, make your wants few."

Old age is a time when the meaning of life shifts from external circumstances to internal character. Joy is more important than happiness. Yet the thief of secularism has robbed joy of its meaning, particularly among the young who are laying the foundations upon which old age will rise or fall. An old hippie, or an old yuppie, is one of the saddest sights in our society. Without having laid the moral and spiritual foundations for aging, they dead-end in the pursuit of happiness and become the personification of T. S. Eliot's "hollow men" (or women) "stuffed with straw." The future bodes dark for the secularist whose life will be prolonged by medical advancement, but whose meaning is dependent upon youth, health, money, things, and favorable circumstances. A generation of nihilists—elderly people whose life is without meaning—awaits us.

The Biblical Corrective

Everything the Bible says about aging contradicts the "Radical Now," the "Radical Self," and the "Radical Happiness" of the secularist. First and foremost is the fifth commandment of the Law of Moses, "Honor your father and your mother, so that you may live long in the land the LORD your God is giving you" (Exod. 20:12).

No one can dispute the fact that parents are priority in the mind of God. Moreover, He will hold us accountable for our attitudes toward our father and mother. *Honor* is His expectation. Doesn't this mean that we are to show them respect, give them love, value their contribution, affirm the meaning of their life, and take care of them in their need? Because God gave the Ten Commandments as minimum moral standards to sustain human civilization, can we not judge the rise and fall of a nation by its attitude toward its aging people, particularly its fathers and mothers?

The fifth commandment has eternal consequences as well. We can expect one of God's questions for us at the final judgment to be, "Did you honor your father and mother as I commanded you?" There will be no fifth amendment for the fifth commandment. Our answer will be either yes or no.

While God's commandment drops like a plumbline of judgment upon us, it also has a connection with a promise that we must not miss. Honoring our father and mother is the commandment that triggers God's promise of long life in the land that He would give to the Israelites. The connection is natural. In the cycle of generations, the length and quality of life depend upon a three-generational mode of compatible relationships among the young, middle-aged, and elderly. Or more specifically, we need the vision of the young, the reality of the middle-aged, and the wisdom of the old to keep a nation on even keel. Our long life, then, depends upon the honor we give to our father and mother as they grow old. Otherwise, we will lose what God has given to us. If God's commandment still holds (and there is no evidence that it has been cancelled), the storm warnings are up for Western civilization. For us to claim the promise of long life in a good land, we must restore the honor of time, love, and meaning to our fathers and mothers as they grow old.

God's promises begin to multiply with age for the person who obeys His laws and does His will. The promises of honor that are given to the aging person include:

- *Long Life:* "And if you walk in my ways and obey my statutes and commands as David your father did, I will give you a long life." *1 Kings 3:14*
- *Youthful Vigor:* "You will come to the grave in full vigor, like sheaves gathered in season." *Job 5:26*
- *The Symbol of Gray Hair:* "Gray hair is a crown of splendor; it is attained by a righteous life." *Proverbs 16:31*
- *The Assurance of Salvation:* "With long life will I satisfy him and show him my salvation." *Psalms 91:16*
- *Divine Presence to the End:* "Even to your old age and gray hairs I am he, I am he who will sustain you." *Isaiah 46:4*
- *Joy in Accomplishments:* "My chosen ones will long enjoy the works of their hands." *Isaiah 65:22*
- *Respect and Relaxation:* "Once again men and women of ripe old age will sit in the streets of Jerusalem, each with cane in hand because of his age." *Zechariah 8:4*

The Gift of Age

Wisdom is the special gift of the aged. An elderly person with the gift of holy intuition and the experience of trial and error is an invaluable asset to any civilization or society, community or church, family or function. Throughout the Bible, the wisdom of the old is honored. Their counsel channels the enthusiasm of the young, and their dreams keep the middle-aged from giving up. But with their wisdom comes responsibility. In Paul's letter to Titus, the apostle sets out the expectations that go with wisdom. A separate list is given for men and women. His bias may be showing because the list of expectations for older men is positive, while his list for older women emphasizes negatives. At the same time, Paul may be recognizing the special and complementary facets of wisdom that older men and women bring to the community of faith.

Older men are expected to be "temperate, worthy of respect, self-controlled, and sound in faith, in love and in endurance" (Titus 2:2). Older women are expected to be "reverent in the way they live, not to be slanderers or addicted to much wine, but to teach what is good" (Titus 2:3). Immediately following these lists, Titus is urged to teach the young men and women the virtues of Christian character with their elders as examples. Although his sexual bias may seem to show in the separate lists, modeling for the young is the common role that Paul identifies for older men and women in the church. Here again is a biblical distinction for aging that separates the body of Christ from the secular culture. While a secular culture casts its older people aside, the church honors them with the role of being spiritual examples for the young. In this light, we must conclude that our aging parents represent an underutilized resource that needs to be tapped for the spiritual life of the church.

I invite you, then, to join me in learning what our parents have to teach us as they grow old. The lessons will come from crisis and conflict, words and example, laughter and tears, even life and death itself. All make up the wisdom we see when our parents grow old.

CHAPTER 3

Knowing When to Step Down
Retirement

Most of us don't know when it's time to step down. We need someone to help us face the truth. How can you help your parents retire with dignity?

In Dad Voorheis's case, you saw the signal in the eyes of his congregation. After forty-four years as one of the most powerful preachers and effective pastors in the conference, Dad saw his sermons begin to take on the tone of a long-practiced routine. One prominent member of the church led a minor mutiny in the congregation and requested that Dad be moved.

News of the rebellion deeply wounded Dad's sensitive spirit. Still young at the age of sixty-five, he had expected to make this parish his last pastoral appointment. Perhaps at sixty-eight, no later than seventy, he would retire voluntarily. Now, however, he had no choice. To remain under episcopal appointment he would have to accept a lesser charge, which had the reputation for being an exit point for pastors who were burned out or used up.

Always before I had come to Dad Voorheis for counsel. This time he came to me. "What do you think?" he asked, "Should I move or retire?" At the risk of our relationship as father and son by marriage, I dared to answer, "Dad, you and Mom have lived for the day when you could move into your own little home that you just bought for retirement. Why not enjoy these years together? You would still get plenty of invitations to preach. If I were you, I would retire."

Those were the words he heard from my lips, but in my mind I pleaded, *Retire, Dad, while you still have your dignity and while you still have options.*

Dad retired. Whether he responded to my youthful advice or to his own Spirit-guided impulses, I don't know. I do know this. Dad lived for twenty-six more years as the pastoral patriarch in his hometown of Spring Arbor, Michigan. He preached when he wanted to, prayed with hundreds who came to his door, and set the tone for the town as he walked the streets of the small college community. Along with all the residents of the village, every entering class of freshmen soon became acquainted with "Brother Voorheis." Well into his eighties, if anyone sympathetically inquired, "How do you feel?" he brightly returned the patented answer, "Finer than frog's hair." Later, when he began to fail physically, he modified his answer, but not his humor, by falling back on the old quote, "I'm still able to take my regular meals." And that he did.

Dad Voorheis died at the age of ninety-one with all the dignity of an elder statesman in the church and with more love than ever. I've often asked myself, "What if he had tried to hang on?" Perhaps his indomitable spirit would have triumphed on the new pastorate. But if not, I shudder to think of the congregation wanting him to leave but hesitating to hurt him. Almost half a century of dignity could have been lost in the subtle signals of withdrawal and rejection. Someone would have had to tell Dad that he was no longer wanted. The effect of forced retirement upon his gregarious spirit might have been a mortal wound. Even if he lived as long as he did, his verve for life would have been blunted, and his continuing ministry rendered far less effective. Dad knew when to quit.

Stepping Down Gracefully

Ever since my experience with Dad Voorheis's retirement, I have been an observer of older people in long-term positions. Out of these observations have come some guiding principles that I recommend for sons and daughters who are asked for advice by aging parents.

Retire while you are still wanted

Tragedy stalks a person who hangs on to a position when he or she is no longer wanted. Men in high positions are especially vulnerable. Over the years I watched a prominent pastor whose personality became the length and shadow of the megachurch that he founded. His preaching attracted people to the church, his gift for remembering names endeared him to every parishioner, and his leadership for a talented pastoral staff exemplified his skill in empowerment. But he overstayed. All of his leadership theory told him to prepare for pastoral succession and then retire. Periodically, he would set the date for his retirement only to claim a crisis as the time came near. Deferral after deferral proved to be his tactic—at the expense of the church, the pastoral staff, and the membership. While the momentum of past years kept attendance up and programs flourishing, behind the scenes the on-and-off again search committee resigned one by one in frustration, the pastoral staff began circulating their vitas, and the lay leaders put the plans for urgent expansion projects on hold. Finally, the pastoral staff and lay leaders dared to ask the question that sounded like heresy, "How do we tell the truth to the pastor without destroying the man?" Because the pastor had gone past the point of no return, the only answer was a clean, surgical cut of truth. While he would be seriously wounded, the blow would not be fatal. He too had a price to pay.

On the other side of the ledger, a prominent denominational executive approached me one day with the flattering question, "Do you think I should retire?" His query came during a general conference of the church after a resolution had been introduced to prohibit denominational executives from being elected to a four-year-term in office after they reached their sixty-eighth birthday. I understood then why he asked me the question. His sixty-eighth birthday fell just a few days after the cut-off date, and he wanted my vote on a "grandfather clause" that would make him an exception.

Immediately I began to relive my experience with Dad Voorheis. The basic issue seemed to be the same. Before me stood an honored man who wanted to hang on after getting a signal that time was running out. He didn't expect me to reject his plea, but I did. Disappointment dropped his eyes and erased his smile when he heard me say, "Our church needs elder statesmen. If you retire now, you will be honored by all and set free to write and speak from experience. I say retire."

A day later he requested a point of personal privilege with the general conference and stood before the delegates to announce his retirement before the resolution could be enacted. With a modest summary of his achievements and a gracious word of thanks to the church for letting him serve so long, he opened up the years ahead with a vision of writing, speaking, traveling, and serving wherever the church might call. A standing ovation brought him to tears and a unanimous vote for "executive emeritus" stood him up tall. Almost twenty-five years have passed. I've never found out whether my words made a difference. It doesn't matter. At last report, he was approaching the age of ninety with his books still selling and his presence still in demand. Thank God, he knew when to quit.

Lengthen your plans with the length of your years
I've learned this lesson from several sources. A Christian business-man took me by surprise when I asked him how he had celebrated his fifty-fifth birthday. "I started making my thirty-year plan," he answered. Suddenly I knew why I had feared the thought of retirement. My plans stopped with my working days.

While pondering this insight, I realized that we Christians should see the plans for our mortal lives extending into eternity, where we will continue to work with meaning and grow as persons. Thirty-year plans for a fifty-five-year-old Christian are not out of order. In fact, they may be too short! Our model for long-term planning should be Enoch, who walked with God on a continuous journey from time to eternity (Gen. 5:24).

Paul Rees is my other model. He died in 1991 at the age of ninety-one. Although our personal contacts were limited over the years, he served as my model for writing and speaking. In 1982, when I became president at Asbury Theological Seminary, Paul Rees had already retired from the board of trustees with the honor of being named a "Life Trustee." He did not attend the board meetings, but he received all of my memos and reports to the trustees. After each mailing, he wrote me a letter of encouragement. Not one of them ended up in the wastebasket because every letter contained a gem of a sentence that deserved preservation for all time. One of those sentences comes to mind. At the age of ninety, Paul Rees had a disabling injury. His body stopped temporarily, but not his mind or his spirit. In his regular letter, he described his circumstances this way: "Life is like a slab of bacon, a little fat and a little lean. This is one of the lean times."

When Paul died, a friend of the seminary sent me an article that he had written fifteen years earlier under the title, "I Shall Go to My Grave." At the age of seventy-five Paul confessed that he was not young, but neither was he "ill . . . morbid or despondent." He only wanted to ring some bells of his strong and persistent convictions. With peerless language and engaging style, Paul Rees struck the bells ten times as he completed the sentence, "I shall go to my grave . . . "

- *Affirming* my faith in Jesus Christ as absolute reality
- *Appealing* for the unity of the church as the "visible community of Christian faith and fellowship"

23

- *Declaring* that only God in his mercy, through Jesus Christ, could save us from our sin
- *Denouncing* legalistic pigeonholes that produce "culture Christianity" rather than the beloved community of the New Testament
- *Exposing* idolatry as one of the most frequent undetected sins of Christians
- *Believing* that the long years of "pulling and hauling" over a "personal gospel" showed myopia on both sides
- *Regretting* that the holiness of motivating love had been missed by so many Christians who debated whether the "wealth of Christlikeness" was open to us as growth or gift
- *Asserting* trust in the Bible, whose authority is not "derailed by a misspelled word or an erroneously translated term or an incorrect date"
- *Expecting* with ardent hope the second coming of Christ while meeting the mandate "occupy until I come"
- *Unshaking* in the confession that "Jesus Christ is Lord."[1]

Can anyone wonder why he lived with the vigor of youth until the age of ninety-one? Paul Rees lengthened his plans for the length of his years. Like Enoch, he walked with God on a continuous path from time to eternity.

Plan your life in chapters

Elton Trueblood, in his autobiography *While It Is Day,* proposes that life is lived in chapters.[2] Looking back on our personal history, we can see that he is right. Infancy, childhood, adolescence, young adulthood, and middle age all divide nicely into sections, with the possibility of intriguing chapter names. Old age, however, tends to be a blur without design, anticipation, or intrigue. If so, we need to remedy the situation. Why not encourage older people to think of the honor of aging by planning and naming chapters for the years of early, middle, and late retirement? In each case new dimensions of body, mind, and spirit await exploration. Even if there is a chapter of physical suffering, the mind can be well and the spirit can grow. Why not envision old age as an adventure rather than an apprehension?

Cultivate interests and develop identity outside the job

One of the false and sometimes fatal notions that aging people nurse is the assumption that new interests and new identities can be established instantly at the time of retirement. How many times have you heard middle-aged people pledge themselves to start new hobbies and assume new roles when they retire? Evidence contradicts their dreams. Unless a person has a hobby before retirement, it's not likely that he or she will start a new one. Likewise, if a person depends upon work for his or her identity, it's not likely that a new identity can be established. Aging, then, is an extension of our ongoing interests and identity just as it is an extension of time and personality.

Good people can get into trouble after retirement if they are married to their job before retirement. I recall an executive who came to retirement age and could not face the prospect of losing his personal identification with his position. He asked for a two-year deferment and got it. Time slid into a third year and he asked for another grace period. When the directors of the company told him no, he left with the bitterness of being betrayed. In retirement, no new hobbies sparked his interest and no new identity could replace the position from which he received his status. Only time could heal the hurt.

Retirement planning begins years before the fact. A child who cultivates lifelong hobbies may become the healthiest retiree. An adult with multiple identities in family, career, church, and community may be the most satisfied person in old age. In any case, the recommendation is clear. As our parents grow old, we need to encourage them to discover and develop a range of interests and diversity of identities. For many, it may be too late, but it is worth a try.

25

Watch for signs of running down on the job

Entropy is the second Law of Thermodynamics. Simply stated, *entropy* means that physical resources run down with use. A similar loss of quality can take place in us emotionally, relationally, and spiritually on the job. Particularly in aging, we must be alert to the signs of entropy; they'll tell us that it's time to change or quit.

Every person has entropic signs that are unique to his or her personality. With aging, the signs will tend to be aggravated as physical energy declines. The following list of entropic signs is in part a personal confession. I have seen these signs in myself. The other part is the result of my observations of people for whom I have been responsible. When people need a rest, a change, or retirement, you will see these signs of entropy:

1. Boredom on the job. Although the person may still be able to function effectively, due to routine and habit, their performance is effectively flat and their attitude is affectively negative.

2. The loss of joy within oneself. In physical health, we know that being well is more than not being sick. So at work we know that doing the job with joy is more than not being bored. Joy is an intrinsic satisfaction that does not depend upon achievements or rewards. When a person loses what the French call *joi de vivre,* "the joy of life," the consequences are contaminating. The person, as well as everyone with whom he or she works or relates, will feel a loss in the quality of life.

3. Small things become big. It's no secret. When little things that we once handled easily take on the magnitude of a federal case, we are in trouble. Of course, aging has a way of magnifying little things. But when the size of the case is out of proportion to the issue, something's gone wrong.

4. Decisions are deferred. When little things become big, we often resort to the tactic of deferral. Decisions that once were made with surgical precision now are put aside with the hope that the issue will fade. Confrontations that once kept relational conflict from festering are now avoided with the hope that the problem will go away. Worst of all, a series of wrong or halfhearted decisions is made, and it creates a muddle of confusion. Especially when the decisions involve the welfare and destiny of people, deferral that leads to muddling borders on the inexcusable.

5. Emotions become detached. Emotional detachment is one of the reasons why businesses prefer that people who quit a job leave as soon as possible. Otherwise, the results can be demoralizing. An employee who burns out or makes a decision to leave invariably reveals an emotional distance from both the job and people. No one can hide such a change of attitude very long. While the person may not say, "I don't care anymore," the limited span of attention, the lackluster eyes, and the lifeless tone of voice betray an early departure. "Lame ducks" who retire on the job are equally frustrating. In fairness to our employer, as well as to ourselves, we need to leave all at once—emotionally and physically.

6. Fatigue after sleep. Of all the symptoms of entropy, this one is the most evident telltale sign. If a person awakens with fatigue after a full night's sleep, the warning light is burning red. The cause may be stress or sickness, overwork or guilt, aging or anxiety. Whatever the reason, fatigue after a full night's sleep is nature's way of warning us against total breakdown.

There's nothing sacred about these six signs of entropy. Perhaps you found your own symptoms on the list. Or perhaps you found the symptom that troubles your aging parents. If so, it's time to act.

Lean into the future

At first thought, lengthening our plans and leaning into the future may seem to be overlapping recommendations. Highly successful executives often climb to the top of the corporate ladder while still in their forties. Their view from the top, however, is not as glamorous as we imagine it to be. Having gained the position as chairman of the board or president of the company, they have no place to go. The tendency is to look back on past achievements and turn inward until alcohol, divorce, drugs, physical stress, and suicidal thoughts take their toll. Special sessions were offered at the Menninger Clinic in Topeka, Kansas, for these victims of success. The therapy was simple: The goal is to get the chief executives looking forward again. Once they do, their vision clears, their energy rises, and their problems become manageable. Leaning into the future is good therapy for all of us, especially for our parents who are tempted to look back or turn inward when they grow old.

Cultivate the inner life

Our aging parents have a choice. They can either turn inward to work out their frustrations, or they can cultivate the inner life to enlarge their souls. With age, the scale tips from the outer life to the inner life, just as it tips from the body to the spirit. It is a sad sight to witness an aging person whose spirit is shrinking. Certainly, it need not be so. Spirituality is a gift of aging, so every encouragement should be given to our parents to cultivate such spiritual disciplines as prayer, Bible study, devotional reading, solitude, fasting, and journaling in order to build the soul, model the spirit, and serve the church as elders of the faith. From them we have much to learn.

Knowing when to quit, then, is more than a brutal exercise to get elderly people out of the way. With adequate preparation, good timing, long-term planning, and loving care, retirement is just opening another chapter in the futuristic saga called "the good will of God."

CHAPTER 4

Severing the Symbols

Independence

> Symbols of independence, such as working, housekeeping, or traveling, help our parents define who they are. What happens when old age takes away these symbols?

Mom and Dad Voorheis traveled from church to church in itinerant ministry for forty-four years in southern Michigan. Contrary to the options that ministers have today, they never owned a home of their own while serving a parish. Not only that, they served in an era when Free Methodist pastors still followed the pattern of early Methodism and moved every three years. So, in forty-four years they lived in fourteen different manses. Their daughter, Janet, who became my wife, remembers that she never stayed in a school more than two years between the second grade and her sophomore year in high school.

In addition to the regular cycle of pastoral moves, the church conference elected her father to the traveling superintendency twice in that period of time. During those stints as superintendent, the Voorheis family visited different churches every weekend. From Friday afternoon after school to late Sunday night after church, Janet spent her preteen years eating, sleeping, playing, and, most of the time, worshipping on the road. To the everlasting credit of her parents, however, Janet never knew the stigma of a traveling superintendent's kid without a home. When I asked about those years without a permanent home, gratitude glowed in her eyes as she reflected, "I remember the mantel clock that we had in our home. Even though we moved from parsonage to parsonage during those years, whenever the mantel clock was in place, I was at home."

Against this background, you can understand the depth of joy that filled her mother when Dad Voorheis bought the "dream cottage" in Spring Arbor, Michigan, for their retirement. The frugality of years paid off when he put down eight thousand dollars cash for a two-bedroom, white clapboard bungalow, located in the side yard of the college church where he had twice been pastor. They lived in the home for twenty-three years after retirement. Then came the call from the visiting pastor who warned us that Mom's attempts at cooking and Dad's efforts at maintenance endangered their home and their lives.

Dad knew that the time had come to move to a retirement village. Mom's advancing senility, however, allowed for no such nonsense. She felt as if she were quite capable of managing the household and would not hear of anyone selling her home "out from under her." When we talked about the problem with Dad and with her, she sat unknowing in the fog of senility. Moments later, when the fog lifted just enough for her to get a fleeting sense of reality, she would cry out in pain, "What's going on? What are you doing to me?" For the first time in my memory, Mom Voorheis displayed an inner rage that contradicted her spirit of a lifetime. Years earlier, after I started dating her daughter, eating her food, hearing her pray at family devotions, and watching her minister in her home, I described her as a woman "who would have been a saint without salvation." Not that she was soft. On a couple of occasions, I saw her eyes narrow and watched her lips pinch tightly together when someone tried to take advantage of her husband or her daughter. Without raising her voice "Sister

Voorheis"—the name of endearment given to her by parishioners—could settle an issue and bring strong men to silence with just a word.

Senility lifted the lid on feelings Mom had never openly expressed. She spoke harshly to me once. After Dad gave me durable power of attorney and agreed that we should sell the family home, the folks moved into an apartment as the entry point in a three-tier life-care system. Daily meals, weekend cleaning, and periodic nursing checks were provided. When they could no longer function semi-independently, second-tier resident care with service would follow until they needed third-tier bed care in the nursing home. To ease the trauma of transition, my wife and I purchased new furniture for the apartment, transferring only a few sentimental items, especially the mantel clock and their favorite chairs. Nothing satisfied. Mom and Dad Voorheis spent nine months of misery in the apartment. Even with their best friends above them, and lifelong ministerial colleagues around them in adjoining units, they found no joy in the new surroundings. As strange as it may seem, the misery ended when Dad fell and broke his back so that the two of them had to be moved into the same room together in the nursing unit. They were more content in their beds with constant care than they were in the apartment that represented their rupture from the cottage they called "home."

A humorous incident first alerted us to feelings that Mom Voorheis had kept bottled up for years. Living in parsonages next to churches for forty-four years and retiring in the front yard of the Spring Arbor Free Methodist Church made the sound of the churchbell second nature to her. As a gentle way of giving the order "Let's get ready for church" to her family, Mom let the sound of the churchbell be the background for her upbeat, motivating word, "I can feel a little bell ringing in my heart when it's church time." Senility changed the meaning of the bell. During one of our Sunday visits to the nursing home, we planned to take Mom to her beloved church for morning worship. As Janet struggled to get her dressed and groomed, the bell that Mom had heard thousands of times began to ring. Picking up the sound, Janet spoke brightly, "Listen, Mom. Is a little bell ringing in your heart?" Her saintly mother scowled back, sliced her hand across her throat like a radio announcer signaling "Cut," and growled, at the same time, "I've had it *up to here* with church!" This was a Mom we had never known.

A less humorous hint at Mom's hidden hostility came out one day when she and Dad were alone in the room. Without warning, Mom grabbed Dad by the arm and yanked him out of bed with an angry yell, *"Get up. There's nothing wrong with you!"* Of course, Dad's broken back left him helpless. He crashed to the floor and lay there until the nurse came by. Mom had become dangerous in her senility, so the doctor ordered them separated. Dad soon required hospital care and died shortly after admission.

Following Dad's funeral, where I preached and Mom sat without recognition or emotion, Janet and I decided to take her to a Bill Knapp's restaurant, where she and Dad ate regularly when he could still drive. As we drove out of town, a voice from the back seat thrust angry barbs at me, "What are you doing? Where are you going? You never tell me anything. You sold my home and now you're taking me away. I'll never go home again." I knew then what the house meant to Mom. For forty-four years she had dreamed of the day when she would have a home of her own. For a quarter of a century she had lived her dream. As the wife of an itinerant minister moving from parsonage to parsonage for so many years, she felt the little house in Spring Arbor symbolized life itself. Senility in its advanced stages could not blot out the meaning of selling the home. She had lost a symbol of life.

Symbols of Life

Mom's outburst set me thinking about the other symbols of life that I had seen in our aging parents. Dad Voorheis had his own symbol. Perhaps again reflecting how little he owned as a minister on the move, he took special pride in his car. A ritual of washing, cleaning, and polishing, combined with the tender care of maintenance, left no doubt about the prize of his worldly possessions. The fact that Mom never drove and Dad never encouraged her to learn preserved the boundaries of Dad's domain. Like Jack Spratt and his wife, he ruled the car; she ruled the house. They got along very well.

At the age of eighty-two, Dad feared that he would fail the test for renewal of his driver's license. For days he fretted, and when the hour came, he broke out with a rash because of nerves. When he passed both the written and driving tests required for a person of his age, he acted like a teenager getting his first license. A long-distance telephone call informed us, a trip to the local post office spread the news around town, and to celebrate, he drove Mom to Bill Knapp's for dinner.

Four years later, he met a reversal. Reaction time had slowed down until Dad knew that he could be a hazard on the road. In place of the old confidence behind his love for driving, emotional fears caused him to limit his driving to shakedown cruises around the block to keep his car in tune. With great reluctance, he confessed that he could not pass the driver's test again, and rather than being embarrassed he announced that he wanted to give his car to a local man who had been Dad's first convert during his first pastorate in Spring Arbor. The man had gone through financial crisis and could not afford to buy a car of his own. How typical! The car that Dad wouldn't let me drive without extensive instructions became a generous gift for a person in need.

Dad made a voluntary decision when he gave away his car. He himself said, "Now I'm ready for the nursing home." The driver's license symbolized a hold on life, not unlike Mom's house. With the license, he maintained a margin of independence, however small it may have been, that gave him a leverage upon life and reason to live.

When I thought about my own mother's last days, I recalled an incident that illustrated her special symbol of life. As her leukemia became acute, she lost the use of her right leg. Most of the days during the last months were spent lying on the sofa. Persons who didn't know her might think that she was too weak to move. My sister and I knew better. Mom lay on the sofa to conserve her energy for church! Twice on Sunday and once on Wednesday night, a friend stopped by to pick her up for the services. Here is where a lasting image sticks in my mind. On my last visit to see her, my schedule required me to catch an airplane on Wednesday evening. "Will you drive me to church on the way to the airport?" Mom asked. She wore a blue coat with a grey fur collar. Ugly bruises marred her legs, and swollen feet wouldn't fit into regular shoes. I can see her now. Giving me a good-bye kiss, Mom insisted that she needed no help getting up the two steps to the front door of the white-pillared church. As I watched from the car, she leaned on the railing for a moment to muster strength, dragged her useless leg up one step at a time, leaned again on a white pillar, and shuffled toward the usher at the door—a gritty example of faith, wearing bedroom slippers to church.

Church served my mother as the house served Mom Voorheis and the car served Dad Voorheis. More than independence hung on these symbols. Once our parents lost the symbols, they virtually gave up on life itself. Why is there so much meaning in a single symbol? The answer comes with the recognition that, bit by bit, their hold on other symbols, which younger people take for granted, had been cut away from them—their work, travel, friends, freedom, money, health, and in the case of children who move from Michigan to Washington state, their family. No wonder they hung on to their last shred of independence. Life is living in small margins as it is. To see that margin narrowed down to one last symbol is a reality of aging which we never expect to happen.

If I could relive those days with our parents, *I would be more sensitive to the symbols of life.* Each of us holds tightly to a number of symbols that establish our identity as persons—our career, position in the family, role in the church, community, organization or club, home, car, bank account, plans and priorities, travel, and health. On and on the list could go. As we age, however, those symbols of independence—interpreted as life itself—are lost, replaced, shifted, and simplified one at a time. Now I see how I might have helped enrich the old age of our parents. My understanding of the meaning of the symbols of life to them and my working through the changes with that understanding would have helped preserve meaning for them and deepened our relationship.

In that context of understanding, *I would also try to identify the vital symbol of independence for each parent.* Our uniqueness as persons puts a premium on some symbol that gives us our independence. For my mother, the church preserved her personhood; Mom Voorheis hung on to her home; my Dad needed work; and "Brother Voorheis" needed a ministry. Long before retirement, the vital symbol of independence can be discovered in our parents. At present, for instance, I am writing this story on a yellow legal pad beside Lake Chelan, Washington. For me, writing is a vacation, and a yellow legal pad symbolizes my independence as a person. My children already have the hint. For my sixtieth birthday they put together a videotape spoofing the idiosyncrasies of Dad. You guessed it. The first frames of the hilarious and humiliating film show our youngest son sitting in a beach chair in swimming suit and sunglasses with a yellow legal pad on his lap and a black felt pen clenched in his teeth to provoke thought. I identify with that picture. Long after I retire, downscale homes, cease travel, and stop tennis, my pad will give me life. I hope that it is the last thing to go.

We don't always get our wishes. If necessary, *I would be ready to suggest substitute symbols of life for my parents.* Retirement, although not usually a negative experience, is one of the symbols of life that may need a substitute for work when the time comes. For some, leisure may be enough of a substitute. For others, it will not do. My seventy-five-year-old insurance agent called me the other day with an idea for an annuity.

"Kelly," I chided him, "You are supposed to be retired."

"I was," he chuckled, "But after a month on Maui with only a lower golf score as my incentive, I came back to work."

My own father had a similar experience. Retirement from work as an automotive engineer quickly bored him, so he got a part-time job as an usher at the spring training camp of a major league baseball team. By contrast, my wife's father retired to an honored role of pastoral patriarch for the village of Spring Arbor. With his role went the reverential title of "Brother Voorheis," which the citizens and students conferred upon him. While we cannot force substitute symbols of life upon our parents, we can anticipate their need for substitutes and encourage their pursuit.

Yet again, when the relentless march of time takes its toll on the symbols of life for older people, *I would try to help my parents hold on to the most vital symbols as long as possible.*

Mom's church, Dad's work, Mom Voorheis's home, and Dad Voorheis's car served as irreplaceable symbols. With the exception of my father's work, I see that they held them as long as they could. Is this part of the reason why Mom and Dad Voorheis lived into their nineties? If my mother had not contracted leukemia at the age of sixty-five, would she have followed her mother into the late eighties with the church as her life? She died early to be sure, but she also lived fully to the end.

I don't know whether or not my father found a symbol of life as a substitute for work before his heart attack. Years later, a stranger heard the name "McKenna" and asked me if I had a relative in Florida who was a minister. "No," I answered. "My father retired in Sarasota, but he wasn't a minister." Coincidence after coincidence fell as the stranger pressed me for details. Finally he concluded, "Your father must have been the same man. He helped me when I was in trouble." To this day I want to believe that my Dad and that mysterious "minister" were one and the same person. Perhaps he found his substitute symbol.

What happens when the last symbol of life is lost? From the experiences with our parents, *I would shift emphasis from the symbol of independence to the symbol of security for their final days.* As the symbols of independence are eliminated one by one with advancing age, they are also simplified. We watched Mom and Dad Voorheis lose interest in their favorite pastimes, such as eating out, watching television, and visiting with friends. Toward the end of their long lives, meaning seemed to be limited to the next meal. In between meals, they subsisted—sitting, napping, and counting pills. When we realized that food represented their simplest pleasure, we did everything we could to ensure quality for their meals. Mom Voorheis could not be fooled. After she could no longer recognize her daughter, she could still taste with disgust a plate of instant potatoes and warmed-over meat. As simple as it seems, a home-cooked meal served as her symbol of satisfaction.

Mom's need for security matched her need for simplicity in her final years. The loss of her home still obsessed her. When the doctor tried to reduce the drugs that kept her passive in the nursing home, she escaped the attendant's eye, walked out the door, and wandered the icy streets without a coat. A long-time friend of the family picked her up and asked where she was going. Memory momentarily filled in the emptiness of her glazed eyes as she explained, "Home . . . I want to go home."

A heavy weight of guilt fell on my wife when she got the call from the nursing home about the incident. We had changed presidencies from Seattle Pacific University in Seattle, Washington, to Asbury Theological Seminary in Wilmore, Kentucky. One of the compensating values of the move was to shorten the distance between Janet and her mother from twenty-five hundred miles to four hundred miles. Regularly, she drove north from Kentucky to Michigan where she would spend two or three days at a time with her mother. Now the question that haunted her dreams became the subject of a family discussion. "Should we bring Mom to Kentucky to live with us?" The doctor doubted the wisdom of a move because Mom's medication required a constant balancing act to keep her someplace between aggressive behavior and mindless existence.

We compromised with an experiment. Mom would spend the Christmas holidays with us, the grandchildren, and great-grandchildren in Kentucky. If it worked out, a more permanent arrangement might be considered. The visit taught us the meaning of security for an aged person who had lost the last symbol of independence. Mom sat blankly in the back seat of the car on the drive to Kentucky. Occasionally she would cast some words into the air—"Where are we going? Who are you?" A preplanned stop at Bill Knapp's for her favorite meal of fried chicken, au gratin potatoes, biscuits and honey, custard pie, and coffee roused neither her interest nor her appetite.

Things got worse when we arrived at home in Kentucky. Mom sank into a vegetative state. Christmas decorations went up, family arrived, carols were sung, presents were opened, and festive meals were served. Mom either stared at the happenings or slept through them. Her only response came when her medication began to wear off. Whoever stood nearby heard her snap, "Where am I? Who are these people? Take me home."

Her reaction crushed Janet. She and her mother had been the closest friends—shopping, dining, talking, and praying together. Secretly, Janet had envisioned the day when she could bring mother to live with us in order to recapture those golden moments. The Kentucky experiment squashed her dream. For the first time, Janet realized that senility had taken her mother from her. Mom needed the twenty-four-hour care and comfort of the nursing home. To impose a similar regime on our home and family would require a shift in priorities from our public role as president and first lady of the seminary. Our teenage son, with his demanding schedule of church and athletic events, would also have to accept the change. Does this sound selfish? Perhaps it is, but there is another question: What would Mom want? Her nature would always answer, "I had my day. Now it's yours. Make the most of your ministry."

Another question is less selfish: What does Mom need? The surroundings and schedule of the nursing home gave her security. The place she feared and resisted had become her home. To put her into the chaos of our family in Kentucky with its nonstop teenage traffic, flexible meals, intermittent travel, and unscheduled guests would have been unfair to her. Reluctantly Janet drew her conclusion: "It'll never work. Mom needs to go home." During the drive back to Michigan, Mom never said a word. When we arrived at the nursing home and took her to her room, she collapsed into her easy chair with a sigh of relief. A minute later, she left us at the sound of a bell. She was home, and dinner was ready. Mixed with our guilt, we felt good. Mom felt better. Security had replaced independence as the symbol of life.

An Unanswered Question

In our case, the ravages of senility settled the question of Mom Voorheis living with us. For others whose parents are in the uncertain time of transition between living alone and needing care, the Mayo Clinic has produced a report that recommends another set of questions that must be asked. Although the report is written from the perspective of an aging parent who is invited to live with children, the same questions need to be asked from the perspective of a son or daughter who must decide whether or not to bring Mom or Dad home to live.

> 1. Does your mother or father really want to live with you? Do you want them to live with you?
>
> 2. Can you afford to have them live with you?
>
> 3. How easily can your mother or father adapt to your family's lifestyle and you to theirs?
>
> 4. Will your mother or father feel like a visitor in your home?
>
> 5. What are the strengths and weaknesses of your relationship with your mother or father? Is it comfortable? Compromising? Emotionally strained?
>
> 6. Can your mother or father continue to pursue the hobbies he or she enjoys?

7. Can your mother or father keep in touch with friends while living with you?

8. How much time does your mother or father expect to spend with you? If home alone during the day, will he or she feel bored, isolated, or depressed?

9. Will your mother or father have a separate room? How much personal space will your parent need?

10. Can your mother or father bring along a favorite chair? Are there stairs to climb?

11. Can your parent keep a car and driver's license? Is she or he willing to ride the bus? Or is she or he dependent upon you for transportation?

12. Can your parent help with cooking, cleaning, gardening, and other chores? Will he or she want to? Will you let him or her?

13. Will your mother or father need help with personal care? If so, is the family willing to accommodate these needs?

14. Can your mother or father help with household expenses? Do you need this help?

15. Can your parent still manage financial affairs? If not, are you willing to assume this responsibility?

Even these questions fall short of a final answer. Two faculty colleagues stopped me in the hall after learning that I was writing this book. Each of them has an elderly mother living in his home. Smiling but serious, they said, "You need to interview us about living with an aging parent. Our stories would make a book in itself." After hearing a sample of those stories from each of them, I realized that they were right. The questions of the Mayo Clinic cannot anticipate the surprises that await both adult children and aging parents who live together under the same roof. For those stories, this book needs a sequel entitled *Chronic Care for Aging Parents.*

CHAPTER 5

Choosing between Parents
Alienation

Many of today's families are fractured. When someone will be hurt no matter what choice you make, how do you choose—and choose wisely?

No decision could hurt me more. Two months after Mom's diagnosis of leukemia, our oldest son (her first grandson) planned to be married in Seattle. I had already purchased an airline ticket for Mom so that she could participate in the proud moment with us. Dad posed a problem. After his divorce and remarriage, he had withdrawn more and more from our family and his grandchildren. Invitations to attend special events in our children's lives had been accepted and then missed for any number of reasons. In fact, the last event of significance that I remember was a junior varsity basketball game back in Michigan in 1963, when Dad and I saw Doug score eighteen points on long shots from his guard position. After we moved to Seattle in 1968, Doug's senior year in high school, Dad never visited us in our new home.

During one of my side trips to visit with Dad while traveling across the country, I told him about Doug's forthcoming marriage. He paused, the silence became awkward, and then he asked rather sheepishly, "Can we come?" "We" tore me apart because he wanted to bring his second wife. I remembered all of the invitations that had been extended to him and our disappointments. Our children no longer knew him. Yet in my deepest longing and daily prayer, I needed full reconciliation with the father who had been my idol, my best friend, and the person who had led me to Christ. Now I realized how completely he had created a new life and a new family.

An ugly picture of conflict flashed through my mind. Where would Dad and his wife sit at the wedding? In the same row with Mother? How would we celebrate as a family at the rehearsal dinner and the wedding reception? Mom's image of loneliness and terminal illness loomed large against the background of these questions. *She's suffered enough,* I thought. *And now her days are numbered.*

"Dad," I said with terrifying resolution, "I think that we can handle it if you come alone, but I'm not going to do anything to spoil the wedding for Mom." Silence again. Finally, Dad answered, with equal resolution, but not without a sting of sadness, "Then I won't come." The hurt will never go away.

Friends have criticized me for the cruelty of my decision. "Separated and divorced parents are common at weddings," they say. Protocol assures proper distance between them and formal procedures keep communication cordial, at least on the surface. Perhaps I used Mom's illness as an excuse for my own emotions, but I think not. Dad's presence would create enough tension in itself, but to think of him and his wife celebrating together at the wedding would have opened all of the wounds that divorce and remarriage had inflicted upon Mother. No fault could be placed upon Dad's second wife. We knew her as a gracious and sophisticated lady. Neither could I fully fault Dad for his request. He had made a new life from which she was inseparable. Still I had to make a decision, perhaps choosing between the lesser of two evils—Mom's hurt or Dad's hurt.

I chose Mom. She relished every minute of the wedding week— the last-minute chaos, the rehearsal dinner, the march down the aisle on the arm of her son, the special flower given to her by the bride, the wedding reception, the honeymoon send-off, and even the cleanup of wrappings and ribbons. Seven months later she died.

Living with Hurt

If current trends continue, a majority of sons and daughters will have to face the issues of separation, divorce, singleness, and alienation from their aging parents. No easy answers will suffice. In some cases, the years of separation may have created two distinct worlds for the parents. Many times when I ask a divorced person about a former mate, the answer "I have no idea" pronounces that person as good as dead. In other cases, an amicable parting has kept the contact alive through the years, even after remarriage. It's in the wide world between the extremes where the problems of aging take on generational conflict. Each case will present its own ambiguity and demand its own special kind of wrenching decision. In the middle ground—between extremes—we are able to recognize principles that will assist those of us who must decide between separated parents when they confront the crises of aging.

For one thing, we know that *aging always calls out a new set of problems for the sons and daughters of separated parents.* No one can anticipate what those problems will be. They may be as simple as communicating a crisis or as complex as deciding how to fund the costs of health care for one but not the other. I can imagine the conflict created if one parent is brought home to live with a son or daughter, and the other is not. Perish the thought that the time would come when decisions about aging parents would sever the ties of trust and love between brothers and sisters. Like the disputes that arise over the assets of an estate after death, more often than not the cause of the family conflict is money.

Closely related to the new problems that aging brings with separated parents is the alert that *latent feelings of the past are bound to surface.* We sometimes forget that old age is an extension of all aspects of a person—body, mind, and soul. Crisis will aggravate the negative as well as the positive parts of personality and bring to the surface feelings that have been held in check just below the level of the conscious. Guilt and hostility, in particular, will appear when a former spouse becomes ill or impoverished. As usual, the children are caught in the middle. If one parent is favored, the old jealousies reappear, and even if the separation or divorce took place years earlier, old age can mean the resumption of competition for the affections of the children, grandchildren, and great-grandchildren.

As the conflict unfolds, *a choice has to be made between parents.* Separation or divorce may have already forced a choice. If so, old age again will reinforce the decision or, in a reversal of events, open the opportunity for restoring a lost relationship. I hoped that my mom's death would draw us closer to Dad. But when he came to Mother's funeral, he left as quickly as he could from the post-funeral gathering. We knew that he preferred the company of his second wife's children, who lived in the area. My hope for a new start went out the door with him. A show of courtesy, not a need for renewed relationships with our family, brought him to the funeral. Instead of healing, the hurt went deeper.

When a decision between parents has to be made, *the moral dilemma will be a choice between lesser evils.* We wish for decisions in which everybody wins, but these are rare in old age. Especially in the volatile and aggravated circumstances of separation and divorce, almost everybody loses. When I told my dad not to come to Doug's wedding with his wife, he lost a chance to be with the family again; his wife missed an opportunity to become acquainted with us; Doug lost the presence of a grandfather whom he once had known so well; Diane, his bride, missed the chance to meet the man about whom she had heard so much; our three younger children lost a contact with their roots; my wife lost the anticipated joy of reacquaintance with a parent whom she had grown to love; and I . . . I lost the strength and presence of a father. With my decision I dug a hole that could not be filled. Only Dad's death left me more hollow. Because of divorce, the generations had passed to me. Emotionally and spiritually, at least, I became "father of the family" before my time. Only Mom won . . . I think.

Even though someone will get hurt, *we cannot avoid making a decision.* A crisis demands a choice. To defer a decision because someone will get hurt only deepens the wound. If and when that time comes for you, as your separated parents grow old, make a quick, clean, and clear decision. There may be no time to pray, so prepare for the moment by exercising the discipline of prayer every day and developing the sensitivity to the mind of the Spirit as a ready guide for every decision.

Not that all doubts will be erased. Ever since I made the choice for Mom and against Dad almost twenty years ago, I have awakened in the middle of the night asking myself, *Was I fair to Dad? Was I honest with myself? Did I act too quickly? Would I do the same thing again?* As case-hardened as it may seem, in the morning when I awaken, I know that if I had to do it over again, I would make the same decision.

CHAPTER 6

Recycling the Generations
Heredity

As old age dawns on each of us, things happen that are beyond our control. How can we prepare ourselves for them, and yet celebrate the good in each generation?

"If this man has a son, warn him." As blunt as the sentence a judge would pronounce upon a condemned man, the doctor attending my father after his heart attack put me on notice. He had just completed his diagnosis of Dad's condition. Despite a medical checkup and a "clean bill of health" six weeks before the attack, the muscle of Dad's heart had closed down for eleven minutes, causing him to lose oxygen to the brain. When the medics "jump-started" the heart again, a strong beat registered Dad's overall fitness, while a flat line on the EKG left no doubt. The brainstem was dead.

My only sister arrived at the hospital first. I was still en route from Seattle to Sarasota when the doctor made his diagnosis. As he walked out of the room where my sister waited, the words of warning were spoken without hesitation, "If this man has a son, warn him." They came to me with the sounds of an early death sentence. With his professional bluntness I felt an eery, extrasensory fear. The doctor had no idea that I existed!

When I heard his report, I angrily suggested that his lack of tact gave him the bedside manner of a barracuda. Later I calmed down and had my first cholesterol check.

Reliving a Relationship

During my childhood and teenage years, Dad served as my personal and spiritual model. I can still see him sitting in the back row of the auditorium when I debated in the regional contest and standing behind the fence when I played tennis in the state tournament. To this day, I don't know how he found time to take off work in the middle of the afternoon, but his presence clearly communicated his priorities. Nor can I forget him coming to school and having the principal page me over the loudspeaker when he found out that I had been paying my paper bills with cash taken from the coffee can where he put the loose change from weekly church offerings. When he impressed upon me the trust that had been given to him as treasurer of the church and the responsibility he had for the cash in the coffee can, I left school and did not return home until I had collected every back bill from my customers. Knowing how I must have hurt my dad punished me more than a physical beating. He had taught me how to build sailboats and model airplanes. He had given me part-time work on mechanical drawings for his company, he had personally introduced me to Jesus Christ, and he had funded all of my undergraduate and graduate school tuition in order to give me the education he never had. Seeing his only son and daughter receive Ph.D.s from the University of Michigan must have been a reward of highest order.

When my sister and I left home, our parents' marriage came unglued. Dad came home late without explanation, often smelling of alcohol. After an embarrassing arrest for drunken driving, his boss gave him notice: "Once more and you're done." Rumors of another woman began to circulate, and Mother's despair became obvious. In

1961, when I taught on the faculty at Ohio State University, Mom drove through the night from Ypsilanti, Michigan, to Columbus, Ohio. A frantic pounding at the door after midnight awakened us to find her on the front porch, face swollen by tears. Hysterically, she announced, "Your Dad has another woman!" The next morning, I found her car half in the street and half on the lawn. She had driven over two hundred miles in a state of shock.

Six months later, in 1961, I accepted my first college presidency at the age of thirty. Desperately, I wanted my dad to share the inaugural ceremonies with me. Instead, he called me one day just after the school year began to ask that I meet him outside of town at a drive-in restaurant. In the parking lot, over the hood of the car, he told me that he intended to divorce Mother and marry again.

For the next fifteen years our contacts were cordial but guarded. Any mention of religion put a strain on the relationship. When Dad's brother, Bob, lay dying of cancer, I tried to minister to him in the hospital. But Dad rebuffed me with a dismissal: "Bob's affairs are all in order." For those fifteen years, we had little personal contact other than holiday phone calls and courtesy visits. Then in June, 1976, after Mom had died, Debi, our oldest daughter, announced her wedding. Immediately, I called Dad to ask, "If I buy your airplane ticket, will you come?" As quickly as I asked, he accepted. "Yes, of course I'll come." Before we hung up, fifteen years of frustrated love and unmet need broke through to the surface and I said, "Dad, I love you." Emotion muffled his words of response. I think that he said, "I love you too." No matter; we both knew that the frayed lines had been repaired by the words of love. Dad's visit to Seattle for Debi's wedding would be a long-awaited homecoming.

Five days later, the fatal call came. A heart attack felled Dad and reduced him to a vegetable. My rage turned against God. While rushing to catch a last-minute flight to Tampa, I kept demanding, *God, tell me why? If you had just waited two weeks, we would have been a family again.* God may have answered, but I refused to hear him. Finally, just before the plane touched down at O'Hare Field in

51

Chicago, the Holy Spirit calmed me down with the message, *Your last words to your dad were "I love you." Even if he came to Seattle, and lived for many years, what more could you say?* I rested temporarily in that truth.

Waiting through the night and morning hours for a delayed flight at O'Hare Field is a modern form of purgatory. I couldn't sleep, so I wandered from terminal to terminal. What happened next must be put in the category of burning bushes, parting seas, and the sun standing still. While sauntering through the aisles of black leather and chrome seats in the terminal, I spotted a yellow paper cutout in the shape of a doctor's old-fashioned satchel. Curiosity prompted me to pick it up, open it, and read the contents. The yellow satchel cutout was a religious tract with nothing more than Psalm 121 printed tastefully inside. I blinked in disbelief. Grandpa McKenna died in 1945 after quoting the psalm with its promise in the last verse, "The LORD shall preserve thy going out and thy coming in from this time forth, and even for evermore" (Ps. 121:8, KJV). When my dad had called the family together for our regular devotional, the day after Grandpa's funeral, I drew Psalm 121:8 out of the promise box before we prayed. I claimed that psalm as Grandpa McKenna's spiritual inheritance to me. Later, I passed it on to our children as "The McKenna Psalm." We quoted it together when leaving on a trip, or when marriage, education, or career moved us across the country. Today, the Bible in our family room always lies open to that psalm. Wherever we go, or wherever they go, the psalm is our bond of love.

How can I not believe in miracles? No one can convince me that my wanderings through the airport to discover a randomly placed tract on one of a thousand chairs can be explained by coincidence. The Spirit of God confirmed the peace that He had given me on the airplane and added the assurance that, despite Dad's condition, the McKennas were together as a family again.

When I arrived at my father's bedside in Sarasota General Hospital, nothing could have prepared me for the sight. Dad's black, wavy hair with its distinguishing gray fringe, his unwrinkled face, and his tan, muscular chest reminded me that he could easily pass for a man in his late fifties. But now the eyes stared without seeing and rolled without control. Foam gathered at the corner of his mouth, and he could emit no sound except a senseless moan. The body belonged to my dad, but the mind and soul were gone. All of my anger flared again. I wept, rebelled, and kicked the wall. Again, God had to calm me down. When He did, I remembered the yellow paper satchel in my pocket. I left the room, went to the nurses' station, and asked for a piece of scotch tape. Opening the tract for all to read, I printed "The McKenna Psalm" at the top and taped it on the light panel above Dad's head. Nothing more could be done—nothing more needed to be done. With a good-bye kiss, I repeated once more, "Dad, I love you," and walked out of the hospital room. By mutual agreement with my dad's wife and my sister, we instructed the doctor to make Dad comfortable but take no emergency measures to keep him alive in the event of another heart attack. A month later, the attack came. No life-saving measures were taken, and Dad died without a trace of human consciousness.

Factors out of Our Control

When Jesus restored Peter to his leadership role, after the resurrection, He also predicted his future. "When you were younger you dressed yourself and went where you wanted; but when you are old you will stretch out your hands, and someone else will dress you and lead you where you do not want to go" (John 21:18). To specify the way that Peter would die, Jesus used the analogy of old age as the time when our destiny is out of our control.

My experience with Dad fits that pattern. As a person who prides himself in problem-solving and decision-making, I was frustrated by the events of Dad's divorce, heart attack, vegetable state, and eventual death. Try as I might, the situation was out of my control. As tough as it may be on us and our egos, sons and daughters of aging parents will find themselves helpless before such forces as the *hereditary makeup of the parent.*

Dad did everything he could to keep fit at the age of sixty-nine. He walked, swam, dieted, and kept his weight down. Six weeks prior to the heart attack, he had been pronounced a "young sixty-nine-year-old" by the doctor. Tests could not predict a "myocardial infraction" in which the heart muscle closes down to cause death and opens up again to conceal any evidence of heart damage in the autopsy. Heredity played the culprit. So when the doctor saw the results, he did not hesitate to send the message, "If this man has a son, warn him."

I got the message. When diet and exercise did not take me out of danger on the cholesterol count, I went to a cardiologist. Hearing the story of my father, and the doctor's warning to me, he wasted no time. "You make my job easy. I'm putting you on the 'big gun.'" He meant heavy doses of medicine to bring my cholesterol down more than a hundred points in three months! At the end of that test period, he pronounced me out of the danger zone but destined me to the medication for a lifetime. While nothing could be done about my father's heart attack, I and my sons must heed the risk of our heredity.

My hands were also tied by the history of Dad's decisions that created *social circumstances out of my control.* Sons and daughters who must care for aging parents, are filled with *ifs. If* only Dad had not divorced Mother. *If* only Dad had not retired so early. *If* only Dad had not taken to drink. *If* only Dad could have come to Seattle . . . *If* . . . *If* . . . *If* . . . Sooner or later *ifs* must give way to the reality of a destiny created by past decisions. Rather than wishing what might have been, our effectiveness as caregivers will depend upon our ability to deal with reality and go on into the future. For me it meant putting aside resentment because of Dad's remarriage and working together with his second wife, who loved him as much as I did.

Whatever happened in the past was out of our control, but we still had responsibility for the present and the future.

The point of control slipped further when I thought about *the timing for life*. Our schedule was not God's schedule. According to my plans, Dad would come to Seattle, be reconciled with our family, and enter a long period in which he and I could go back to capture the moments of fishing and golf of which divorce had robbed us. Out of those special times, then, I envisioned a conversation about spiritual matters that would bring Dad back to Christ and a profession of faith. None of this happened. The time of Dad's heart attack, hospitalization, and death were out of my hands. I could only submit to God's timing and help make the small decisions about time in intensive care, the move to a nursing home, and the order against other emergency measures. How arrogant it is to assume otherwise. We are pretenders to the throne of God when we declare our sovereign right to decide the birth or death, abortion or suicide of a person. If my experience has any carryover value, I believe that the best-laid human plans for the timing of life will be frustrated by God's surprises. When all is said and done, we will learn that He is in control.

Make no mistake: God's control of the timing of life is positive, not negative. From firsthand experience, I am glad to report that *the work of the Holy Spirit in the lives of aging parents is also out of our control*. Never again will I presume that God needs me to get His work done. I'll go a step further. God's will in the life of my father is better than my best-laid plans. This cannot be said without the perspective of time. I'm sure that my plans for our reconciliation and redemption resulted from my best thinking and deepest love. But they must be checked against the facts of history. I found out that Dad set the condominium community in Florida buzzing with his excitement about his pending visit to Seattle and Debi's wedding. As my last word to him, I said, "Dad, I love you." A tract imprinted with "The

McKenna Psalm" appeared for me on a seat in the airport, and mercy kept Dad alive until I could unite our family under the promise "The LORD shall preserve thy going out and thy coming in from this time forth, and even for evermore."

As my heritage, Dad left me a warning, and God gave me a promise. What more can I ask?

CHAPTER 7

Parenting Our Parents

Roles

When aging causes parents to act like children, children must act as parents. Are we ready for the reversal?

"Dad, I've had it. Quit bugging me. I mean it, now!" My wife's voice exploded just below the level of a scream from the downstairs family room. A second later, she appeared at the top of the stairs in a flood of tears.

"I can't believe it," she said, choking, then continued, "I've never talked to my father like that."

The explosion had been building for several days. Her father and mother were visiting us in Seattle for the last time. Dad Voorheis was eighty-seven years old and Mom Voorheis was eighty-three. Each showed evidence of old age: Dad had a disfiguring nervous disease, and Mom showed the first signs of senility. When Dad declared, "This will be our last visit," our intuition told us that he spoke the hard truth.

Due to my stupidity, the trip started off as a disaster. I had driven the seventy-mile run from Spring Arbor, Michigan, to the Detroit airport a hundred times during my years as president of Spring Arbor College. Precise timing required an hour and fifteen minutes for the drive, twenty minutes to turn in the rental car, and ten minutes to the gate, in order to arrive in time for the boarding call. When I traveled alone, I allowed for no margin of error. Occasionally, I hit the gate as the door closed—but I never missed a flight.

Two unforeseen events upset my timing. First, the state of Michigan had just enacted a law that reduced the speed limit on the interstate from seventy to fifty-five miles an hour. Second, I hadn't counted on the extra minutes to check Mom's and Dad's bags, get them to the Red Carpet Room of United Airlines to wait for me, turn in the car, return by bus, pick them up, and walk them slowly to the airplane. Needless to say, I missed the flight.

Three hours of waiting faced us. Dad and Mom had already expressed their anxiety about the flight, and now, thanks to me, they couldn't even trust their son-in-law. Amidst all of my self-flagellation, Dad and Mom gave me a moment to remember. After two hours of mock confidence in which I told them several times, "Don't worry, the name of the game in air travel is 'hurry up and wait,'" I walked them to the gate an hour ahead of the flight time. A convenient bench behind the agents' counter became our roost for an hour. Of course I got antsy and had to make a telephone call.

"Sit right here," I instructed them, "I'll call home, and come right back."

When I returned, Mom and Dad sat like models for a Norman Rockwell painting. Imagine this beautiful white-haired couple in their mid to late eighties, holding hands for me to see, and grinning from ear to ear like children who just skipped school without getting caught. To break the tension, they pulled the prank that they had been planning for the trip. When they held up their clasped hands, I saw the sparkle of a diamond and a wedding band.

My face showed the shock they wanted to see. Old-time Free Methodists, especially pastors, never wore wedding bands, to say nothing about diamonds. Dad had done his share of preaching against "gold, pearl, and costly array." In her tasteful but plain dress, Mom could never be accused of "superfluous adornment." Yet there they sat, flaunting the diamond and giggling like kids. Dad's good humor spoke the punchline. "We were worried that someone would see us traveling together and think that we're not married."

Mom held the ring up for my inspection. I could only ask, "Where in the world did you get it?"

"Out of the box on the dresser," Mom answered matter-of-factly. "Thirty years ago, when Mary Cummings was converted under Dad's preaching, she took it off and left it on the altar. It's been in the box ever since." Through humor, Dad and Mom revealed their return in fantasy to younger days with their unfulfilled wishes.

Soon after Janet's parents arrived in Seattle from that trip, we encountered the downside of their return to younger days. In the first hints of Mom's oncoming senility, she forgot facts recited minutes earlier in a conversation, but remembered details in her childhood with frightening lucidity. Dad took another turn. Ten years earlier, he had shown some signs of senility—primarily forgetfulness. The doctor discovered some "sludge" in the carotid artery feeding blood to the brain. With what the doctor called a "roto-rooter" he performed surgery, which set the blood flowing freely again. We could not believe the difference in Dad. Mentally, he became as sharp as he had been in his fifties. All traces of memory loss disappeared, and he returned to the preaching for which he was known—quoting Scripture, hymns, and poems at length.

Medical science deserves rave notices for its works of wonder. But we sometimes forget that the human body is so finely tuned that positive change in one part can trigger a negative change in another part. How else can we account for the fact that Dad Voorheis became a young mind in an aging body? As the body aged and weakened, his mind rebelled against the facts, and he began to resent his aging. True to his personality, however, he directed his resentment toward others with a "nervous Nellie" demand on details. Mom Voorheis, of course, became his first victim. His demands upon her were impossible, and she, true to her personality, retreated within herself, rather than rebel. Independently, my wife and I came to the conclusion that the onset and advancement of Mom's senility correlated directly with Dad's surgery and his subsequent demands. As we often said, "If we could put his mind and her body together, we would have one young parent."

Once in Seattle, Dad's obsession with details affected our entire family. The airline tickets became his case in point. From the moment he arrived, he demanded that my wife get the return flight confirmed, even though the time was two weeks away. Janet said, "I'll do it, but there's no hurry. Twenty-four hours in advance is plenty of time." Still, Dad did not let up. Each day began with the question, "Did you get our tickets fixed?" Persistence became an obsession. Finally, a full week before the flight, my wife could take no more. She exploded, "Dad, I've had it. Stop bugging me. I mean it, now!" The reversal of roles almost unbalanced my wife. A life of obedience to her father had been broken. As she told me later, "It was almost more than I could take. Our roles were reversed. I was the parent and he was the child. I never spoke to my father that way."

Masters of Manipulation

Sons and daughters of aging parents must be ready for the reversal of roles. There is no way to escape the shock of change. After a lifetime of listening to the instructions of parents, it is unnatural to give commands with the voice of authority. Yet there is no alternative. Older people are masters of manipulation. They have a full quiver of arrows to shoot and get their way. Guilt is their favorite weapon. One day my wife took her mother out of the nursing home and away from her father for an afternoon of the kind of leisurely shopping that had bound them together for so many years. When they returned, Dad Voorheis complained, "Because you were gone, the nurse wouldn't give me any dinner." In disbelief, my wife went to the nurses' station to ask if Dad had dinner. Of course he did. His complaint of neglect was nothing more than a manipulative tactic to make his wife and daughter feel guilty for going shopping.

Before condemning our aging parents for using many childish tactics to manipulate us and get their way, we must remember that their repertoire of influence has been severely reduced. At the same time, they usually know what they are doing. Delbert McHenry, psychology professor at Seattle Pacific University, opened a new world of understanding elderly people in his studies at a nursing home.[1] A resident incessantly called, "I want my mama," until an attendant became exasperated. "Stop it," the attendant countered, "Your mother has been dead for twenty years."

Shock covered the woman's face. Dropping her head, she confessed, "I know it. I was just trying to get your attention." Her confession so piqued Dr. McHenry's research mind that he did an intensive study on the behavioral effects of aged persons being relocated in nursing homes. He found that the expectations new residents brought to the nursing homes directly affected the relocation stress they experienced. Negative expectations were created when the new residents felt as if the move to the nursing home meant a loss of independence or inability to control one's environment, rejection by children, or prelude to death. The often-used tactic of getting Mom or Dad to "try out" the nursing home as an experiment also worked against a positive adjustment to relocation. As might be expected, the best adjustments were made by aged persons who were still relatively healthy, mentally active, and free from neurotic defenses against stress. Neurotic coping mechanisms that the aged persons used to deal with stress prior to admission became especially pronounced in reaction against the new environment. Resorting to defensive or manipulative tactics, they withdrew from mental activity, such as reading, writing, and hobbies, isolated themselves from other people, neglected grooming, and stopped eating or picked at their food. Not surprisingly, they lost memory, became confused, and often suffered premature death.

Not all of the adjustment to relocation rested upon the expectations of the elderly person. The environment of the nursing home itself tended to reinforce the new resident's expectations. On another occasion, Dr. McHenry met a new resident who likened the nursing home to a prison. When asked why he felt this way, the man answered, "They won't let you come or go when you want to." A few weeks later, Dr. McHenry was visiting the nursing home again when word spread that the man had disappeared. A search of the buildings started when Dr. McHenry remembered their conversation and suggested that they alert the police for a search of the neighborhood. Within minutes the police found the man walking on a street several blocks from the nursing home. When the man came back through the door with a police escort, he spotted McHenry and gave him a knowing look. "See, I told you it was like a prison. When you go for a walk they send the police after you!"

McHenry's recommendations from the study should be implemented by cooperative agreement of aging parents who can participate in the decision for relocation, their adult children or family, and the staff of the nursing home itself:

> 1. Aging parents and family members need an orientation program that educates them on the realities of nursing home life and assists them in developing constructive strategies for dealing with the stress of relocation.

> 2. Administrators, nurses, and support staff need in-service training on understanding new residents' expectations and modifying policies that might adversely affect their adjustment.

> 3. Applicants for nursing home care should be diagnosed for dominant personal characteristics that might affect their adjustment and should be placed in a nursing home environment that can respond positively to these characteristics. The mismatch of residents and nursing homes is often the cause of severe stress, neurotic defenses, manipulative techniques, and even premature death.

While we must be aware of the coping mechanisms used by our aging parents and avoid being intimidated by them, we cannot lose compassion for their plight.

Dad Voorheis used on me the same technique of badgering that had driven his daughter to a violent outburst. During a visit to their home in Spring Arbor a few months before we were forced to move them to the apartment, Dad said that he had to get the garbage can out on the curb for the weekly pickup. "I'll do it, Dad," I volunteered. My wife interrupted to say that it was too early to put the garbage out. The day was Tuesday—the pickup was Friday.

On Wednesday morning, Dad responded to my "Good morning," with an oblique reference to the garbage can. I ignored him. So on Wednesday evening he spoke with urgency, "We've got to get the garbage out." Disgusted now, I snapped back, "Look Dad, I said I'd get the garbage can out in time, and I will. *Relax.*" Still my wife recommended that I get the can on the curb the first thing on Thursday morning. I did my job, but did it wrong. After I put the can on the curb, Dad went out and shifted it over to the "right spot" for the pickup. When he came back into the house, I jumped at him—"Dad, you created a crisis with that garbage can and upset the whole household. Why?"

Momentarily returning to the pastoral tone that he had used to calm so many distraught parishioners, Dad answered, "Son, someday you'll understand. When you get old, even the little things are big." From then on, I tried to see the world through his eyes before reacting. When the manipulation was obvious, I had to be firm. When the tactic was desperate, I had to be fair. And in either case, I had to try to understand. What appear to us as games that our aging parents play may well be the only way they can cope with the passing of life, over which they have little control.

CHAPTER 8

Borrowing on Trust

Finances

"Just don't report it. The government owes it to you anyway." I didn't expect to hear such words from a Christian attorney. After listening to my troubling questions about funding the cost of the nursing home for Mom and Dad Voorheis, he recommended that we cheat! How would you respond?

At the time, we had a year or more until the move to the nursing home had to be made. Financial questions, however, pressed upon us. Dad and Mom had never written a will. In fact, they served as ministers in a era when written wills were thought to betray a lack of faith. For persons who had always depended upon God to take care of them, the idea of protecting their limited assets and passing them on to their children contradicted a lifetime of trust. Still, Dad's conservative nature had permitted him to save the cash to buy a retirement home and retain a small nest egg in long-term low-interest bonds. The home, the bonds, and the personal property of the car, furniture, and clothing, when added together, made up the sum total of their estate.

Friends of Mom and Dad had already moved to the retirement village with subsidized rentals or to the nursing home under Medicare. When we began to inquire about the qualifications for financial assistance in these facilities, the answer confused us. Some of the residents qualified by poverty. Others still owned homes, which they rented out. And still others had children controlling the wealth that they had amassed in their lifetime. Only a few seemed to pay the full price of monthly care.

We needed counsel, so I found a Christian attorney whom several of the residents had retained. He listened carefully as I presented our case and ran down my prepared list of questions. He recommended that Dad and Mom prepare a will—a formidable task in itself. Then he proposed that Dad and Mom might start giving their assets to their children and grandchildren in order to reduce estate taxes and qualify eventually for rental subsidies and Medicaid.

"What about the home and car?" I inquired.

"Well, this is the gray area," the attorney answered. "You can keep your house without penalty if you intend to return to it and your car if you will drive it again. Who knows? To answer your question, I would say, just don't report it. The government owes it to you anyway."

Planning Smart and Playing Fair

I left the attorney's office knowing how people beat the system. Even Christians can rationalize cheating the "federal monster" in the gray areas of the law. To hear this from a reputable Christian attorney, however, disheartened me. I vowed then and there to become a student of the law and the system in order to help Mom and Dad Voorheis. One caveat would rule: *Whatever we did would be within the law.*

A written will became the first order of business. How would I be able to convince Mom and Dad Voorheis that provision for the future did not constitute a lack of faith? The argument about the government getting their money wouldn't work. They didn't feel as if they had enough to matter. The same thought countered the motive to leave something to their children and grandchildren. The breach of faith and the hassle of a legal document mattered more than an inheritance. After weighing every option, I concluded that my only alternative was to test the trust that we had built in each other as in-laws. A hazard loomed. No matter how much our love and trust might have grown over the years, was there an inherent suspicion that a son-in-law might have been pursuing his own interest?

I took the chance, but couched my recommendation in a package of mutual need. My wife and I also needed to have our will updated to correspond with the different needs of our married and single children. A visit to another attorney assured me that Dad and Mom's will would be very simple. So armed with the information, I approached Dad with the plan. "Janet and I need to have our will updated now that two of the children are married. While I was with the attorney, I asked if a will for you would be complex. He said 'No, it would be very simple—at most a page or two.' So your Scotch son-in-law asked if he could do two at once. 'Sure,' he said, 'I'll do two for the price of one.'"

"What do you think, Dad? Should I have him do it?"

A frown, a thought, and probably a prayer, swept across Dad's face before he answered, "Okay, if you think we should. I'll have to talk Mom into signing it."

Initially Mom protested, but with Dad's urging she signed the simple will, dividing the assets equally between my wife and her older brother after their parents died.

Another crisis loomed. The local church offered to buy their house, which stood in the front yard as a visual barrier to the new sanctuary and educational unit. The thought of selling the home panicked Dad. So with the consultation of an attorney, I developed a plan for the folks to give the house to the church in exchange for low-interest bonds. Their taxable income would accrue to the children until the bonds matured, at which time the principal would be divided equally between Janet and her brother. To complete the transaction, however, I needed to have broad and durable power of attorney in order to protect Dad from the details. *Broad* power of attorney would provide me with the legal authority to borrow or give money, purchase items or property, file tax returns, and execute trusts and legal agreements; *durable* power of attorney would let me continue as "attorney in fact" if Dad became incapacitated and could not act for himself. Trust again came into play. With a word of confidence and a sigh of relief, Dad gave me the broad and durable power of attorney to make the decisions in accord with his wishes and to his and Mom's benefit. His show of trust is a commendation I cherish.

Next, we had to determine how to handle the remaining assets. As mentioned earlier, he gave away his car to a convert of his ministry who needed transportation. The bonds, which he had kept since Depression days without reinvesting the earnings, remained a problem. A check on the law informed us that a person who qualifies for Medicaid had to be limited to a very small bank account and burial insurance one year in advance of eligibility. Dad and Mom's specter of the "poorhouse" darkened my mind. To be eligible for Medicaid, a person had to be impoverished. But there was another side to the dilemma. If our parents still held the bonds as assets, they would have to be spent first and none of Dad's years of savings would benefit his children. Hobson's choice stood before us. Either give the bonds away to the children and claim poverty for the parents, or use the bonds to pay the nursing care cost for about one year and then plead poverty. In the latter case, the children would get nothing from the estate beyond the church bonds from the house.

Not wanting to use my power of attorney for a decision of self-interest, I laid out the options for Dad. Giving him the vow that we would always give him and Mom first-class care, whatever the cost, I told him that he could divide the bonds now as specified in his will to the benefit of the children, or take the risk that they would be used for taxes or for nursing home expenses until exhausted. He asked, "What would you do?"

"I've always planned to give something to our children and grandchildren," I answered. "Tax laws permit you to give gifts to them, so I'd have the joy of giving to them while I'm still alive."

"I agree. Let's do it," Dad decided. True to my prediction, he found great joy in cashing the bonds and writing the checks in small thousands to grandchildren just starting their homes and to his son and daughter as a gift of his love.

Time became our ally. Dad completed his gift program exactly twelve months before the nursing home decision had to be made. Although the laws may vary from state to state, when we applied for Medicare and filled in the sections about income, home, car, investments, pension, bank accounts, life insurance, and burial coverage, he and Mom qualified for full medical care based upon full reporting. Legally Mom would be classified as living below the poverty level, but in terms of the quality of total care in a Christian nursing home, she enjoyed the comfort and security that is wealth for an older person. At the same time, Dad Voorheis died with the satisfaction of helping build his church, while giving gifts to his children and grandchildren that helped buy first homes, fund graduate study, and start bank accounts.

Map Work in a No-Man's Land

Memories of those moments make me shudder. Overnight I found myself thrust into a fuzzy financial world with no clear markers and no easy answers. Although I felt the burden of responsibility for our parents' welfare, I didn't even know which questions to ask. By trial, error, and providence, I learned enough about financial planning to map out a course of action. At the very least I learned to ask these questions:

1. Where is your parents' financial information, including everything from hidden documents in lock boxes to complicated contracts, agreements, and trusts?

2. What is their financial status—assets, liabilities, and net worth?

3. Who is their attorney, tax accountant, and financial consultant, if any?

4. Do they have an up-to-date legal will on file?

5. Have they developed a financial "nest egg" over the years? How are the funds invested? Has the financial plan been adjusted for retirement?

6. Have they given broad and durable power of attorney to a family member or a professional confidant?

7. Have they made plans for their assets to minimize estate taxes?

8. Are they receiving full entitlement for their Social Security benefits?

9. What are the provisions of their pension plans and life insurance?

10. Do they have adequate medical and hospital insurance, including catastrophic coverage and long-term care?

11. What are the monthly budget requirements to sustain a reasonable standard of living for them?

12. Are they eligible for Medicare? Medicaid? Do they carry Medigap insurance?

13. Have they made funeral arrangements and purchased a cemetery plot?

14. If worse comes to worst, what are the contingency plans for financial shortfall or catastrophe?

No claim is made for the comprehensive coverage of these questions. Retirement manuals provide a better list, and financial consultants know every detail. For my part, I want to make a case for estate planning for Christians as an extension of biblical stewardship. Startling statistics show that a majority of Americans die "intestate," or without a will. Older Christians may add to that number by feeling as if a written will represents a lack of faith in God. They may resist the idea of using a legal will as an instrument assuring the pattern of their Christian stewardship after death. But each of us should consider the consequences of leaving our assets to the discretion of the federal government. If, while living, we tithe our income, add offerings of gratitude to God, sacrifice to support faith ministries, and give gifts to our children, it is inconceivable to think that death reverses the pattern and refutes our purpose. Although it may be too late to change the perspective of aging parents whose lifetime of success with economic conservatism limits the risk of shifting resources and exercising creative options, nevertheless, we should approach them with the question, "What are your wishes for your assets after death?" If they desire to continue their support for the family and their stewardship for the church, the way is open to discuss the provisions of their will or to engage a financial consultant who is particularly sensitive to Christian concerns. If our parents resist such a question, it is better to back off and pray that the Holy Spirit might open their minds to new truth, even in old age.

For those of us whose children will be our caregivers in the future, we need to espouse the biblical principle of Christian stewardship for life and for eternity. Someone once said, "The real test of stewardship is our checkbook." I would add, "The ultimate test of stewardship is our written will." As our checkbook reveals our current priorities for ourselves, our families, and our God, our will puts the stamp of the future upon those priorities.

No financial formula will work for all aging parents. Differences in individual personalities, family relationships, financial assets, and state laws are enough to create an infinite variety of patterns to which sons and daughters must respond. Whatever the pattern, however, one common element will determine the quality of the outcome. That element is a "long-term trust" developed prior to the crisis of aging, active when the difficult decisions hang in the balance, and continuing to give assurance until death. Trust is the basis upon which assets are revealed, wills are written, power of attorney is granted, financial plans are accepted, assets are liquidated, and quality life-care is assured. Without that trust, money can be the monster that causes suspicion, divides families, wastes assets, and leaves our parents living with unavoidable miseries of old age. Sad to say, the Christian faith of parents and children does not guarantee the trust needed to deal with the financial dilemmas of aging. While we need to see faith as a resource upon which trust is built, it still takes time and it must be earned. Old age is the test of that trust.

CHAPTER 9

Handling Our Emotions
Guilt

No matter how much we love our aging parents, we can never do enough. Guilt, whether fact or fantasy, will be a part of our emotions. Can this guilt be forgiven? Can we forgive ourselves?

As I look back upon our experiences with aging parents, I realize guilt could have become a demon to haunt us and a club to cripple us.

Guilt comes in many packages, individually wrapped for each of us. In our case, I can identify four reasons for the guilt that we had to handle.

Guilt from decision
When my mother's leukemia advanced into the acute state, she entered the hospital in Ypsilanti, Michigan, for the last time. I called her doctor from Seattle, Washington, to ask if I should fly immediately to her side. He responded by saying that he did not expect imminent death but would keep me posted on her condition with the assurance that I would have time to make the flight.

Later that evening, I received another long-distance telephone call from the nurse who was attending my mother. She reported that her bedside experience with leukemia patients gave her reason to believe that Mom would die before the night was over. The conflict between the professional opinion of the doctor and the personal experience of the nurse tore at my emotions. If Mom should die, I wanted to be at her bedside. If she continued to survive for days, I had the pressure of long-standing commitments for year-end ceremonies at the University. I decided to accept the doctor's opinion and wait through the night.

Hindsight says that I should have followed the heart of the nurse rather than the head of the doctor. Mom died in the night, and I felt the guilt of failure as her only son. If I had to do it over, I would have delegated my presidential duties and taken the "red-eye-special" across the continent to be with her.

Guilt by transfer

My father's heart attack left him "brain dead" in Sarasota, Florida. In his case, the doctor urged me to remain in Seattle until the weekend because he could give no hope for my father's recovery. Again, I accepted the doctor's professional judgment.

Dad's youngest sister, however, flew from Phoenix, Arizona, to Florida the moment she heard the news. Arriving in Sarasota, she went to the hospital and found him in an agitated state with his eyes rolling and his arms flailing against the restraining straps. After he calmed down, she tried desperately to communicate with him by speaking family names and familiar words. Occasionally an involuntary movement gave her hope, but in the end, all of her efforts proved futile. Late that night, she called me on the telephone to report on her visit. Speaking through tears, she drove a stake into my heart: "I am convinced that he is waiting for you to come," she said. "That's why he is so restless. If you spoke to him I know that he would respond."

As Dad's only son who felt estranged from him for fifteen years and then experienced the joy of reconciliation just before his heart attack, my vulnerability was laid bare. Of course, I hurried up my schedule, took the "red-eye" from Seattle to Sarasota, and went directly to my father. Alone with him, I whispered my name, recited "The McKenna Psalm," and sang "Jesus Loves Me." The doctor was right. Dad showed no sign of human consciousness. My guilt turned to anger, and I kicked the wall as I left the room.

Guilt from delay

Five years later, Janet's ninety-one-year-old father fell and broke his back. After a long period in the nursing home, it became obvious that he would not recover. Finally, the doctor ordered him into the hospital, where he lingered for several days. Janet followed his condition daily by telephone calls to her brother. He assured her that he would call if Dad took a turn for the worse. Ironically, the same pastor who had called three years earlier to urge us to move Dad and Mom Voorheis from their home before they hurt themselves called again. This time he urged Janet to come to her father because he saw life ebbing away. She already had her suitcase packed, but with children still at home she had to take another day to arrange for meals and appointments. Dad died just hours before she arrived.

Guilt from regret

Two years after her father's death, Janet confessed that she hid within herself the guilt of not being with him when he died. The confession came out when she talked with me about her dream of having Mom Voorheis live with us if Dad died first. She and her mother especially enjoyed shopping together. Janet anticipated serving her mother full-time and taking her to the mall for an afternoon of bargain hunting. By the time Dad died, however, senility had already taken its toll upon Mom. Her lifetime love for shopping disappeared along with her loss of recognition for friends and relatives, including her daughter. In her moment of confession Janet spoke her regret, "Perhaps I could have done more to help Mom with the stress of caring for Dad."

Our Natural Ambivalence

We cannot escape guilt in caring for our aging parents. No matter how much we try to do for them, it is never enough. Part of the problem is the tension between their needs and our needs. As aging parents require more and more care, we must give up time, money, and energy that would have been used to meet our own needs. Ideally, we might say that Christian love for our aging parents is an "unlimited liability" without boundaries or conditions. Realistically, however, we bump into boundaries and confront conditions that require choices and cause guilt.

In Robert Wuthnow's book *Acts of Compassion,* he notes that our desire to show compassion for others often conflicts with our need for self-fulfillment.[1] An example might be a daughter who defers on a graduate degree in her profession in order to care for an aging parent. Or, in our particular case, we felt conflicting pressures to care for our parents and fulfill God's calling to presidencies in Christian higher education. More often than not, we must try to balance these conflicting demands on the fulcrum of our motives. When Janet concluded that she could not bring her mother to live permanently with us, her love for her mother did not diminish. In fact, I would argue that she loved her more because she gave up her own desire for the sake of Mom's safety and security. If she had insisted on caring for her mother at the expense of her family and our ministry, her guilt would have been compounded and, ironically, Mom would never have known the difference.

Good News for Guilt

From our experience, some guiding principles evolve for dealing with the guilt that comes from conflicting motives when we care for aging parents.

First, our best is never good enough. If guilt comes because of decisions we must make about caring for our parents, then guilt is inevitable. Aging is a process filled with surprises that we cannot anticipate and circumstances we cannot control. Like the best-laid plans of mice and men, care for our aging parents can go astray. Even our decisions require a choice between two "greater goods" or two "lesser evils." When Janet made the choice for our family and our ministry over the full-time care of her mother, she still had moments when she second-guessed her own decision. Even then, the greater danger is to let guilt dictate our decisions. We can do too much, too early for our aging parents so that they become dependent upon us. Our guilt may be relieved, but at the price of their independence and dignity.

Second, we cannot brutalize ourselves with guilt. If, in caring for our aging parents, we lose our individual identity, stunt our personal growth, hurt our family relationships, or cripple our professional effectiveness, we must ask the serious question, "Is there a better way?" Something is wrong with any relationship in which one of the parties is smothered by love or smothers with love. If we make our parents overdependent upon us, it is wrong. In either case, a neurotic need is being met under the guise of loving care. Whether in parent-child, husband-wife, or child-parent relationships, mutual needs must be met and mutual growth must be the goal. When God commanded us to "honor our father and mother" He did not mean that our care would be crippling for either parent or child. Here is where our motives come into play. If our decisions are motivated by love for our parents and esteem for them as persons, we should be relieved of debilitating guilt.

Third, others cannot judge us. As I recall the episode with my dad's youngest sister, her shock at seeing my father's unseeing eyes rolling in his head and his frothy tongue hanging out of his mouth drove her to desperation. Faulting me for not coming instantly to his bedside, she put on me the onus for his recovery. I do not blame her. One look at Dad, and I too lost my composure in a fit of anger. At the same time, when I saw his condition, I felt some resentment against Dad's sister for judging me and making me feel guilty. A few hours together with her restored the lines of love we had always known as "favorite aunt" and "favorite nephew." Still, I came away from that experience with the firm conviction that no one should pass judgment on children who are doing their best out of the motive of love and with a desire to dignify their parents.

Fourth, God's grace forgives our guilt. Even after we have done our best and worked through the downside of our decision in caring for our aging parents, guilt can remain. Also, when we look into our motives, we will often discover a conflict between love for our parents and love for ourselves. Or we may see that we diminished their dignity by making them overly dependent upon us. Whatever the reason for our guilt, God's grace is sufficient. According to Scripture, the worst sin is to curse our parents (Matt. 15:4). Another sin is to "mock" them (Prov. 30:17). Still another sin is to "dishonor" them (Deut. 27:16), and another is to "forsake [their] teaching" (Prov. 6:20). All of these sins are worthy of punishment ranging from death to the displeasure of God. If we are guilty, we must ask forgiveness of God and our parents.

Old age is special in the mind of God. As children who love the Lord and our parents, the guide for our decisions should be the spirit of the law more than the letter of the law. God speaks in that spirit when He says, "Rise in the presence of the aged, show respect for the elderly and revere your God. I am the LORD" (Lev. 19:32). Note the word *and*. It is what Elton Trueblood calls a "holy conjunction" linking two interrelated and inseparable thoughts. "Show respect for the elderly *and* revere your God" leaves no doubt. The quality test for the care of our aging parents is the "respect, dignity, honor, and esteem" that our decisions give to them. Even now, I remember Janet's decision to pay extra each month to have her mother's hair done in a beauty shop until the day she died. Visitors remarked about the beautiful white-haired lady sitting in the hall, and the nurses said that her face seemed to shine after her hair was done. Is such a simple gesture of respect for a parent equal with our reverence for God? According to His Word, it is. If we respect our parents and revere our Lord, grace will cover the guilt that comes when we try to second-guess ourselves with the questions "Did I do my best?" and "Did I do enough?"

CHAPTER 10

Meeting Our Mortality
Sickness

All of us are living on borrowed time. But that is no more acute than in an aging parent who has been diagnosed with an illness from which he or she will never recover. What can you do for an aging parent in this situation?

"Dr. McKenna, Dr. McKenna. Please go to a white courtesy phone for an emergency call." Imagine being greeted with this message from an overhead speaker just as you stepped off the airplane in a distant airport. A myriad of morbid thoughts tumbled through my mind as I scanned the concourse for an all-white phone. The sign of one on a far wall brought me to the edge of panic. Was my wife in an accident? Was one of our children killed? Or was it a disaster at the university? I readied myself for the worst news but didn't expect to hear the choked and teary voice of my only sister. "Mother just came back from the doctor's," she reported as calmly as she could. "The diagnosis is leukemia—chronic now, but the kind that advances rapidly to the acute stage. She has nine months to live."

How did I respond? Denial is the usual reaction to news that we cannot comprehend. As if to doubt her words, I asked, "Are you sure?" Before she could answer I corrected myself and shifted my doubt to the diagnosis. "Is the doctor sure? Should we get a second opinion?" My sister quickly convinced me that a team of doctors had conferred on the test results and concurred in the diagnosis. I went on, "How is Mom taking it?"

"You know her," my sister answered. "She has faith for healing."

Our conversation closed with the agreement that I would soon come home to see Mother, but not on an emergency schedule that could make death seem imminent.

Life took a new turn for mother and for us. I lived in Seattle, Washington, twenty-five hundred miles away from Ypsilanti, Michigan. My sister lived in Detroit, just thirty miles away from Mom. The burden for care, of course, fell upon her. Still, as the only son and eldest child, I sensed both the weight of giving support and the guilt of having moved so far away. I recalled Mom's puzzled comment to my sister after she had visited us in Seattle. "When is Dave going to settle down and come home?" Although she had a childlike faith that could not be broken, she never fully understood the call of God that took her son to Seattle—a distant mission field would have made more sense.

Grace and Grit

Mom's singleness following divorce multiplied the complexity of the problem caused by the diagnosis of leukemia. After the divorce in 1962, she had lived alone in the family home and survived on the low wages of a food handler on the cafeteria line at the local university. Her Finnish ancestry added a stubborn edge of independence to her existence. She lived within her meager salary, traveled far and wide with a woman friend, never missed church, and found high adventure in pageants, parades, religious concerts, theme parks, and evangelistic services. In the next nine months, however, everything would change. Frequent trips to the doctor to monitor her blood count would keep her close to home. Anemic symptoms would weaken her body until new blood could be transfused. With the weakening would come other breakdowns that would hospitalize her or require extensive therapy. Then, without a miracle, the inevitable would happen. One of the tests would show a jump on the leukemic scale from "chronic" to "acute." The higher the mark on the scale, the shorter the time until Mom would die—most likely from secondary causes brought on by a weakened body that could fight no more.

What do you do for an aging parent who is living on borrowed time? Immediately, you do nothing but build the hope and foster the faith for healing. Mom became our first priority for daily prayer and the object of our commitment to spare no medical means for her to beat the statistics. Then we encouraged her to keep working as long as she could, and take the vacation time due her for a trip to Seattle and a visit with her grandchildren. The memory of that visit is bittersweet. Mom wanted to do everything that she had always done—walking two miles around Queen Anne Hill, stopping for doughnuts, shopping for the grandchildren, and attending University functions with us. Although she acted as if her introduction as "President McKenna's mother" meant nothing to her, deep down we all knew that the woman who dropped out of school after the eighth grade basked in the glory of her role as the "First Mother of the University."

Early in her last Seattle visit, she announced a lifetime desire to climb on Mt. Rainier. Her wish became my command. Cancelling all appointments on the first clear day, and gathering the two youngest of our four children, we drove up the mountain as far as we could. After lunch in the lodge at Paradise, Mom wanted to test the trails leading up the mountain to Camp Muir. A very short hike brought the excursion to an end. When we arrived back at the lodge, Mom had developed a discernible limp. Although she rejected any help, my wife and I cast a knowing glance at each other. The first symptom of a weakening body had appeared.

By the time Mom got home, the right leg had lost all strength. Hours of therapy followed in which she had to reverse the habit of a lifetime and learn to walk upstairs leading with the strength of the left leg. During this time, she never lost her sense of humor. "To think that these legs used to dance," she said, as she dragged her useless foot up one step at a time.

When Mom mentioned dancing, she lifted the curtain on the drama of her personal history that only the grace of God can explain. Born Ilmi Elvira Matson in a Finnish colony in Hibbing, Minnesota, she moved with her parents to an equally sheltered Finnish colony in Fitchburg, Massachusetts, where she spoke only Finnish until she went to school. Except for funerals and weddings in the transplanted state church of Finland, her religious training was nil. Her boiler-making, good-natured, and alcoholic father stumbled home after hours in the local pub. Except for his hatred of the godless Bolsheviks who had raped his homeland, Grandpa Matson prided himself in agnosticism.

Dropping out of school after the eighth grade, Mom, her sister, and two cousins left the Finnish colony and sought work in the "land of opportunity." To cover her ethnic ancestry, Mom changed her name from Ilmi to Helen. Then, after being shunted from menial job to job in Fitchburg, she and her sister and cousins took their chances in the glamour of the city—beginning in Boston and ending in Detroit. Dancing and breathing went together for these young women. In Boston they auditioned for the Ziegfield Follies and, when they failed, began to work as "taxi dancers" in the dime-a-dance palaces of Boston. Taxi dancing also paid their bills when they migrated to Detroit.

Mom never told us the story of dating Dad and getting married. We only knew that a taxi dancer and a Greyhound bus driver met in a dance hall and were hastily married by a justice of the peace on an unknown date. Not until my father announced his plans for divorce and remarriage thirty-two years later did I know that my conception led to their wedding.

Six months after my birth I also led them to Christian conversion. The doctor told my mother that my life hung in the balance of a twelve-hour overnight period. If a blood clot went to my heart, I would die. If it traveled past the heart during the night, I had a chance to live. With Dad on the road driving his bus, my mother called in desperation to Grandma McKenna. Although she had no faith herself, Mother knew that Grandma prayed. Later, Grandma told me how she stayed on her knees all night long, praying for me, dedicating me to the work of the Lord, and receiving the promise of my healing. All of her prayers were answered, and Mom became a believer. Dad soon followed, and together they gave my sister and me a Christian home throughout most of our growing years.

Tension between our parents intensified as my sister and I passed through our high school and college years. Once we were married and gone, nothing remained to hold our parents together. Separation followed by divorce left Mother alone to fend for herself. A house, a small alimony, and a cafeteria job made her a survivor. You can see why the diagnosis of leukemia put an ironic touch upon Mom's later years. At the age of sixty-five she deserved the joys of home, husband, family, and church. But she never screamed at God, "Unfair." I, her son, did it for her.

Seven months after Mom's initial diagnosis, she rode a physical roller coaster from transfusion to transfusion. Her employer had granted her a medical leave, and trips out of the house became less and less frequent. Only once did I see the evidence of desperation in her faith. On one of the visits that I planned when traveling across the country, I found the form letter from a faith-healer thanking her for her ten-dollar gift and assuring her that God had heard his prayers on her behalf. Healing was guaranteed. At first I rebelled against the thought of my mother being duped by a faith healer. But the wise Spirit of God stopped me from scolding her. Mom had the right to grasp for spiritual straws. If I had been her, I might have done the same thing—or worse. My anger shifted to televangelists who perpetrate the scam that bleeds desperately ill people of these subsistence dollars. In my mind they should be targets of the same rage that caused Jesus to condemn the scribes who "devour widows' houses."

When I last visited Mom, she could barely walk. I suggested that we could go out for dinner, but she insisted that my sister and I go without her. "No way," I persisted. "We want you to be our special guest for Alaskan crab legs, your favorite dinner." That did it. Mom laboriously got dressed and appeared as well as she could with the black and blue bruises of leukemia showing on her arms and legs. When we arrived at the restaurant, she protested my ordering a full dinner for her. "Oh, I can never eat that much," she said. But when the dinner came, she didn't stop until every shred of meat had been picked from the shells.

"How about dessert, Mom?" I suggested after the entree had been devoured.

"Oh no, I can't eat another bite."

"But Mom, this place has the best reputation for apple strudel in the whole state of Michigan."

"Well, if you put it that way. You get dessert and I'll take a taste."

When the dessert came, I put the apple strudel in front of Mom and watched it disappear. I didn't get a bite and couldn't have been more satisfied. Mom's last meal with her children is a memory that will last forever.

The dreaded day arrived. Mom entered the hospital for a transfusion that didn't take. Instead she became weaker and weaker until consciousness faded. My sister called again with the news that life could be counted in hours—too few for me to reach her bedside from Seattle. So, with just a sigh, Mom died—exactly nine months from the date of her diagnosis.

Caregiving for Chronic Illness

What did we learn from the experience? What can we pass on to other sons and daughters whose parents are growing old? If chronic disease and its inevitable end become the burden that we must share with our parents, my advice is to:

1. Keep hope alive at all costs.

2. Support the risk of experimental treatment.

3. Put top priority on being with them.

4. Engage them in family affairs.

5. Fulfill their lifelong dreams.

6. Tap the resources of their memory.

7. Be patient in their desperate moments.

8. Celebrate their simplest needs.

9. Talk eternity freely with them.

10. Assure them of their lasting legacy to you and your family.

Speaking of a lasting legacy, Mom left us one that is written on a piece of paper no larger than a memo pad. I found it in her Bible after she died. Nine items are listed with a check mark beside six of them. It was her daily prayer list. At the top I found my name and the notation of a career decision that I had to make. Next came my sister's name along with the name of her husband. The single word *marriage* served as a reminder of marital difficulty. Our oldest son, Doug, got on the list as he left for graduate school in Minnesota. Other names appeared that I did not know. Most likely they were friends from work or church. One prayer reminder particularly tickled me. Mom had been praying for "Hazel's knee."

The check marks brought tears to my eyes because I realized that each of these prayers had been answered—my career decision, my sister's reconciliation with her husband, and Doug's graduate school adjustment. No check mark followed the prayer for "Hazel's knee," but knowing of Mom's faith, I told myself with utter confidence, *Whoever Hazel is, her knee is healed.*

In a small way I tried to honor the legacy of faith she gave to me when I dedicated to Mom my book entitled *The Whisper of His Grace.* On the dedicatory page you will read,

To My Mother
A taxi dancer transformed
into
A saint of God.

Now you understand why.

CHAPTER 11

Dealing with Doubt
Salvation

When an aging parent dies without a clear confession of faith, you are left with a myriad of unanswered spiritual questions. Is it wrong to hang on to the threads of hope?

A nightmare in the daytime still haunts me. Soon after my sister and I graduated from college, married, and set up our own homes, the flaws in our parents' marriage split into fissures of irreconcilable differences. Dad had entered a pattern of nights away from home punctuated by drinking bouts that caused him to become sullen and noncommunicative. My sister suffered through these years because she lived close to our parents and stayed in constant contact, while I lived in Columbus, Ohio, two hundred miles away, and made visits once or twice a month. For me, the full revelation of marital breakdown came shortly after I returned to Michigan in 1961, to assume the presidency of Spring Arbor College. Dad asked me to meet him at a drive-in restaurant outside of Jackson, Michigan. Looking across the hood of his white convertible, he got right to the point, "I'm divorcing your mother."

Keeping my composure, I asked, "Is there another woman involved?"

"Yes," Dad confessed. "Although that's not the major reason for the divorce. I haven't told you before, but I only married your mother to give you a name."

Anger must have flushed my face as I fired back, "Dad, you can't hurt me now. I'm my own man."

When Dad did not answer, I kept the initiative by asking a prickly question, "What about Christ?" Like Peter of old, Dad uttered his denial, "I never knew Him. All of those years . . . I was playing a game."

With the memory of him meeting me at the altar when I went forward to confess my sins and invite Christ into my heart, I fired a parting shot: "I'll never believe that for one minute. You were my model, and you led me to Christ." Spinning on his heel, without a word he walked away and essentially out of my life for the next fifteen years.

During those years of estrangement, my father and I never talked about religion. We both knew that the subject would only widen the gap between us and close down even the niceties of superficial conversation. I suspect that the subject haunted him as it did me—always lurking just beneath the surface and keeping us from talking about anything more than golf and grandkids.

Even though I finally told my Dad "I love you" just a week before his fatal heart attack, he died without us ever talking religion again.

How do you handle the death of a parent who has either denied the faith or refused to accept Christ? Our emotions immediately collide with our reason. Each of us wants to claim eternal life for our parents whether or not they openly professed their faith and lived a Christian life. Yet our theology makes it clear that those who die in their sins without Christ are lost. In my case, I could not get over Dad's denial of Christ in the Faustian setting of a parking lot at a drive-in restaurant. As far as I was concerned, he might as well have drawn three circles on the ground and sold his soul to the devil.

In the days after Dad died, I searched in desperation through my memory for the slightest hint of faith restored. His return to church as an Episcopalian and faithful service as a warden in that church helped some, but not much. The bias of an early age held fast. I reasoned that he became an Episcopalian to justify his divorce, cigars, and vodka. Not content to leave the matter in God's hand, I needed a stronger thread of evidence upon which to hang my hope.

God surprised me. Not one, but three threads of hope were given to bolster my hope in Dad's salvation. Although I wish that he had confessed his faith to me in order to cancel his denial, I understand how he might have felt compelled to speak the right language and do the right things to convince me. Instead, he left me with three surprising threads of evidence that I have woven into the confidence that Dad died in Christ.

The Thread of Scripture

I tugged with hope on the first thread as Dad lingered as a vegetable in the hospital. When I was lunching with my stepmother between hospital visits, she went into the bedroom and brought out a dog-eared and khaki-colored copy of a soldier's New Testament. A jackknife was strapped to the book by a rubber band. Immediately I recognized the blade that Dad had used to teach me how to carve a whistle out of the green twig of a willow tree.

"I know that your dad wants you to have these," my stepmother explained. "He read the Bible every morning of his life."

Totally taken by surprise, I could only mumble "Thank you" and flip through the pages with the hope of finding a marked passage. There were none, but the frayed edges assured me that Dad had read the Word over and over again. Although the New Testament and a pocket knife constituted the sum total of my material inheritance from

Dad, it was enough. He left me a thread of hope to believe that he did in death what he could not do in life—let me know that his denial of Christ was a temporary lapse for which he repented and from which he had been restored. Later, when I wrote *The Communicator's Commentary on the Gospel of Mark,* I discovered the depth of Christ's forgiving love in a phrase that is easily overlooked. After the Resurrection when Jesus sent Mary Magdalene, Mary mother of James, and Salome to the disciples with instructions, He said, "But go, tell his disciples *and Peter*, 'He is going ahead of you into Galilee. There you will see him, just as he told you'" (Mark 16:7, emphasis mine). To single out Peter by name is the special invitation that always comes with Christ's forgiveness. Otherwise, none of us would blame Peter for assuming that Christ's instructions to His "disciples" did not include him because he had denied his Lord and violated His trust.

Because of the New Testament that is still in the top drawer of my desk, I believe that when Christ instructs His disciples to meet Him, He will add a special invitation to my father by saying, *"and Loren too."* Come to think of it, isn't that the personalized invitation on which we all must count? Who has not sinned and come short of the glory of God?

The Thread of Prayer

Another thread of hope became woven into the first one at Dad's memorial service in the Episcopal church. When the priest gave the homily, he recalled a pastoral visit with my father within days of his heart attack. As the conversation during this pastoral visit turned to spiritual things, the priest remembered one sentence that he used to eulogize the life of my father. Dad told him, "When I can't sleep at night, I don't count sheep. I talk to the Shepherd."

Again, my mind groped for understanding. Was this the same father who had told me not to pray at his dying brother's bedside? Was he playing word games with the priest, or was God giving me another thread upon which to hang my hope? Ever since that memorial service I've regretted my reluctance to go to the priest and press him for details. Then again, maybe I didn't want to know more. If I had forced Dad's words into the mold of my expectations, I might have found reason to doubt the sincerity of his confession. God Himself seemed to tell me to leave well enough alone. A thin thread of hope is far better than no thread at all.

The Thread of Witness

Now I had two interwoven threads upon which to build my hope in Dad's salvation—reading the Bible in the morning and praying to God in the night. I held on to these thin threads for more than ten years after Dad's death. Then the puzzle took a twist that either closes the case or compounds the mystery. While I was speaking at a leadership conference for life-fitness managers in Orlando, Florida, a delegate came up to me and asked, "Are you related to a Mac McKenna in Sarasota?" I told him that my father, whose friends called him Mac, had retired in Sarasota but died more than ten years ago. The man admitted that he hadn't seen "Mac" for many years, but remembered him among the retirees of Sarasota as "the preacher." While I fumbled with my doubts about my Dad being identified as "the preacher," and not knowing whether the title meant ridicule or respect, the man went on to recite instances when "Mac" spoke his faith to others, gave comfort to men in crisis, and often offered grace at public functions. Other than that, the man knew little about "Mac McKenna"—not his first name, his address, or his career before retirement. Even when I described my Dad in detail, he varied between "Yes, that sounds like him," to "I don't really remember." A shroud of mystery fell over my anxious questions. Was I chasing a ghost? Finally I realized that the man had nothing more to offer. Based upon circumstantial evidence, "Mac McKenna," known as "the preacher" in Sarasota, Florida, might well have been my father. Only faith can see in this incident another fragile thread of hope that reaches across the gap between my father "the prodigal" and my father "the preacher."

Three threads of faith make a strong strand of hope. Woven together, they make a composite memory of my father as a person who not only read the Word and prayed to God but practiced his faith in word and deed among his peers. Aren't these the qualities we expect of a Christian? For me, only the retraction of his denial of Christ is missing. But who am I to assume that he owed me his confession? Perhaps I am part of the problem.

With this insight, I leave my father's eternal destiny in the hands of a loving God. Of course, my most fervent prayer is that I might have had full assurance of Dad's salvation. But I am also willing to rest on the weight of the posthumous evidence. Certainly, if the scales of divine judgment were tipped on the side of the evidence, I believe that Dad confessed Christ and entered His presence at the time of death.

The Stories of Others

Since grappling with the facts, faith, and even fiction regarding Dad's salvation, I have paid close attention to the stories of other persons whose aged parents died without the full assurance of their salvation. It is an understatement to say that once you become sensitized to this question, you find person after person who lives daily with the same doubts. Within the short period of two weeks, I heard three colleagues speak their hurt of living with alcoholic fathers who died with their salvation in doubt. One colleague told of his compulsion to return to his hometown. When he arrived, he learned that his homestead, filled with memories of his drunken father's abuse, was scheduled for demolition. As he collected artifacts of his boyhood home, he forgave his deceased father for all the physical and emotional abuse that he had suffered. In his case, he needed to forgive his father after death without knowing whether or not his father had ever asked forgiveness of God.

Another colleague spoke her despair after scheduling a visit to her home at Christmastime with the intention of telling her alcoholic father that she loved him despite the fact that he had rejected her and abandoned the family. Before she arrived, however, her father died tragically in an accident along a freeway. In a drunken state, he had stalled his pickup truck on the road, pulled over on the shoulder, and, ironically, was hit by another truck that went out of control. When I asked her if she had any evidence that might suggest repentance, she sadly shook her head and said, "No, I've had to work through all of my feelings after his death."

Still another colleague told a more hopeful deathbed story. His father lived into his mid-seventies without a change from a lifetime of spiritual skepticism and substance abuse. Lung cancer, a natural consequence of chain-smoking, caused the man to review his life and his relationships. Step by step, he rewalked the path back toward reconciliation with his children and his God. When the cancer spread and death neared, my colleague traveled to Florida to visit his father one last time. After a cordial visit that kept distance between father and son, my colleague said good-bye and left the hospital. On the way to the airport he felt compelled to turn around and go back to the hospital in order to hug his father and say "I love you." Although he sensed that both he and his father wanted to express their love in those last moments together, a show of affection had become so alien to them that neither could make the first move. As with all of us, my colleague will live with the regrets of not following his impulse. Instead of turning around, he went on to catch his plane and await word of his father's death.

The bad news came to him framed as a good-news story. His sister stayed with their father during his last moments. Shortly before his death, when he was too weak to speak, he kept pointing a finger upward toward the ceiling. No one could figure out the meaning of the gesture until the sister concluded that he was signaling his readiness to go home to heaven. Taking him in her arms, she whispered, "Daddy, it's all right. You can go home now." Instantly he relaxed, fell into a peaceful sleep, and died in her arms. Although my colleague had to accept the substitute of his sister's arms for his final hug, he rests in the assurance that a finger pointed upward signaled "All is well."

A Theology for Doubt

Are there any principles that we can draw from these varied experiences of children whose parents died without a formal, public confession of faith in Christ? As I have reflected upon my own experience, and added the perspective of others, I come to these guiding thoughts for those who must live with the same question.

Be a Wesleyan regarding the work of the Holy Spirit in the lives of aging parents who are nonbelievers. As an alternative to the theology of Calvinists, who preached that those whom God elected for salvation or damnation were categorically either in or out of the kingdom, John Wesley offered the theology of "prevenient grace" with the meaning that the Holy Spirit works in the lives of nonbelievers, "nudging" them toward salvation in Christ. Whether he used the term or not, C. S. Lewis personally illustrated prevenient grace in his autobiography *Surprised by Joy* when he remembered the small encounters with the Spirit of God that eventually led him to Christ. Most of us will identify with similar encounters in our own spiritual journey. When we recall all of the providences that led us to Christ, prevenient grace is the best description we can offer.

Why not watch for those "nudges" of the Spirit in the lives of parents who are nonbelievers? Although the satisfactions may be small, we cannot let our impatience short-circuit the work of the Holy Spirit. My guess is that the most difficult case for evangelism is between a child and a parent. To confront a parent with the claims of

Christ and ask for a decision may be our driving desire, but the reversal of roles may be more than either we or our parent can accept. The situation may be analogous to the physician who tries to treat his or her own family: The loss of objectivity can hinder healing. Evangelism may require some objectivity as well. We may know how to lead our parents to Christ, but our emotions can get in the way. Furthermore, we must assume the Holy Spirit can do His work without us. While we need to be ready for the divine moment if the Holy Spirit beckons us to stand at the intersection for our parent's salvation, our first course of action is to pray for the evidence of "prevenient grace" at work in their lives and then rejoice in the knowledge, however small it may be, that the Spirit of God is nudging them toward redeeming grace.

Be an optimist as you weigh the evidence of God's grace at work in the lives of aging parents who are nonbelievers. Pessimism is the natural reaction to parents who seem trapped in years of skeptical disbelief or sinful habits. As we learned in introductory psychology, the personality of a child is permanently shaped by the age of eleven or twelve. Add the cardinal rule that executives use in selecting their staff, "Past performance is the best predictor of future performance." Mix in Jeremiah's question, "Can the leopard change its spots?" (Jer. 13:23, paraphrased). Fill out the picture then with the findings of chaplains in hospital settings. By and large, deathbed conversions are temporary responses to panic. Most often, the onset of illness only speeds a person along the path they have walked for a lifetime. If they are religious, their faith deepens; if they are secular, their stoicism gets stronger. The sum total of these predictors is pessimism about the salvation of parents who come to old age without confessing Christ.

Only the grace of God can make the difference. All of the predictors that lead to pessimism are human. They are not false, and, if limited to the human dimension, they are true. Divine grace, then, is the intervening variable that changes the equation in favor of optimism rather than pessimism. By faith, we can believe in grace and see every evidence as an affirmative sign pointing to hope despite the odds from a human perspective. Never give up hope. Grace is the free gift of God that we can neither earn nor predict.

Be a Calvinist regarding the will of God in the soul of the nonbelieving parent. No matter how strong our faith or how confirming the evidence, we must ultimately commit the eternal destiny of our parents to the good will of a loving God. Jesus spoke that trust in His final prayer from the cross, "Father, into thy hands I commend my spirit." With that declaration of trust, He covered every contingency of limited knowledge and lingering doubt. We must do the same with our parents when clinching evidence of salvation is not in place at the time of death. "Father, into your hands I commend their spirit" is the declaration of trust in the sovereign will of God, which we cannot second-guess. Each of us must count on grace and mercy to give us the benefit of the doubt.

Be a realist regarding the truth that salvation is in Christ alone. Truth does not contradict grace in the will and work of God. However strong our desire to wish a nonbelieving parent into the kingdom of God, we must hold on to the inescapable truth that there is no salvation outside of Christ. Otherwise we find ourselves on the slippery slope toward universalism, which cancels the scandal of the Cross. While we may not know whether or not a parent, such as my father, trusted in Christ alone for his salvation, we do know that our hope turns on that confession. If so, we may have to resign ourselves to a dilemma that will never be resolved this side of eternity. On one horn of the dilemma, we exercise the faith that finds hope in bits and pieces of evidence that grace was leading our parent to Christ. On the opposite horn, however, we cannot neglect the reality of God's truth—there is no salvation outside of Christ. Once the dilemma is posed, we must then rest in the promise that in God's providence, both truth and grace will prevail.

CHAPTER 12

Sightings of Heaven
Death

> When death comes to claim our aging parent, what promises can we cling to? There is one foundational truth: The path that we walk in life will be the same path that we walk into eternity.

No one expected Mom Voorheis to outlive her only son, Eldon. After early retirement from an industrial position in middle management, Eldon settled into the role of a full-time husband, father, grandfather, and son. A bout with emphysema put him in the hospital during his middle sixties, but only his wife and children knew about the panic attacks in the night when he would be choked awake for lack of breath. Otherwise, he appeared lean and young for his age.

Eldon's retirement routine included weekly visits to the nursing home in Spring Arbor, Michigan, where Mom Voorheis "hung on" with a strong heart in a frail body and a failed mind. Janet, my wife, counted on those visits from her only brother to monitor Mom's condition because distance limited her to quarterly trips from

Kentucky to Michigan. Inbetween, she and Eldon communicated by telephone to make sure that all of Mom's needs were met.

For more than half a century, Mom Voorheis had prayed for the salvation of her son. Eldon lost his first child and only daughter to an acute attack of leukemia, which took just three days to ravage a chubby two-year-old and cause her death. Eldon's faith never quite recovered from the shock. Outwardly, at least, he never professed his faith, even though he listened with full respect when his father preached or his mother prayed. Senility robbed Mom Voorheis of seeing her prayers answered for the salvation of her son. Even when we took her to the college church where she and her husband had ministered for many years, no sign of recognition broke through as we entered the sanctuary, sang the hymns, uttered the prayers, heard the sermon, and greeted lifelong friends at the doors. As best we could tell, Mom's faithful prayers for her son had disappeared along with all other conscious memories in the dense fog of her senility.

One act of providence taught us how wrong we were. It all began with a telephone ringing in the distance of our dreams. As the sound got closer and grew louder, Janet pinched me. "Dave, get the phone. It's Mom." She had told me about her premonition that we would hear of her mother's death by telephone in the middle of the night. Now we knew the time had come. I picked up the receiver, mumbled a sleepy "Hello," and heard the person on the other end of the line identify himself as Eldon's son, Roger. "Dad just died" he reported with the bravado required of the oldest son when the cycle of the generations turns to put him on top. Bit by bit, the story unraveled. Eldon had died in his sleep. After surviving an attack of emphysema earlier in the night, he died from a weakened heart.

Two days later, the remnant of a small family gathered for the funeral. When we arrived in Michigan, Janet asked me to take her first to visit her mother. A body diminished to less than ninety pounds and sustained by spoon-feeding lay motionless on the bed. Long ago, Mom Voorheis had lost the light of recognition from her eyes. When Janet bent down, kissed her, and said, "Mom, it's Janet," unseeing eyes gave no hint of response. Still, when I arrived at the room after parking the car, a resolute daughter greeted me with the declaration, "I'm taking Mom to Eldon's funeral tomorrow." I did not argue. Janet had inherited her mother's gracious but gritty spirit. Only once or twice in forty years had I heard either of them speak with the command of a military general. But when the order came, everybody marched—including me. So I could only watch in awe as Janet arranged every detail from finding Mom's missing glasses to assuring the nurse that she could help her mother walk up the stairs of the funeral home.

Wind and rain added misery to our grief the next day. Janet countered with contingency plans for a raincoat, umbrella, and permission to enter the funeral parlor by the ramp at the side door. When she finished curling Mom's hair and touching her cheeks with a tinge of rouge—a taboo among Free Methodist preachers' wives in her generation—not even Mom's vacant stare could blur the beauty of the woman we had known. I pushed her in a wheelchair to the door and then held an umbrella overhead as she shuffled a few steps to the car, where I slowly turned her around, sat her down, and lifted her feet into the back seat. All of this went on without a word from Mom. A few months earlier, she would have asked incessantly, "Where are we going?" "Who are you?" and "What are you doing to me?" Now we sensed a major triumph to have her in the car, even if it meant attending the funeral of her only son.

We arrived at the mortuary just a minute before the service began. All of the efforts to get Mom into the car were reversed to get her out. The rain continued to fall as Janet coaxed her step by step, helping her to shuffle up the ramp used for wheeling caskets to the hearse. When we entered the side door in full view of the seated mourners, an audible gasp of mingled surprise and joy could be heard. I knew then the reason for Janet's resolve. Mom Voorheis symbolized the family. Even though she did not know us, we needed her—to remember who we were, why we came together, and what we believed. Without the presence of Mom at Eldon's funeral, we would have

101

floundered helplessly in our grief. But as we sat her down between us in the front row, we knew that we were ready to meet head-on the reality of unexpected death.

The brief service began as all funerals do—prelude, prayer, obituary, and tribute. In closing, the pastor invited us to hear God's Word of comfort in the Twenty-third Psalm. The moment he began to speak the familiar words, "The LORD is my shepherd; I shall not want . . . " another strong and clear voice took over the lead.

It was Mom!

I looked to my right and met Janet's eyes glistening from the left. In the middle we saw Mom, no longer slumping almost lifeless in her seat. With the posture of a queen, her eyes shone with beatific vision and her lips moved with the surety of a saint. By now, a crescendo of voices from a funeral chorus of rejuvenated mourners rose to follow her:

> Yea, though I walk through the valley of the shadow of death,
> I will fear no evil;
> For thou art with me;
> thy rod and thy staff they comfort me,
>
> United in new hope, we declared our faith together,
>
> *And I will dwell in the house of the LORD forever.*
> Amen. KJV

With a blessing and a benediction, the simple service ended. Eldon's wife and two sons went first to the casket and wept together their farewell. Mom, Janet, and I came next. Holding Mom between us, we waited while she sorted out the scene in front of her. Finally, her eyes fixed on the face in the casket.

"Is that my boy?" she inquired.

"Yes, Mom," Janet answered. "That's Eldon."

A reflective pause, then Mom asked, "Is he in heaven with Daddy?"

Janet paused for a moment as if gathering her faith and checking with God. Tears almost broke her voice, but with certainty she spoke. "Yes, Mom, Eldon is in heaven with Daddy and Jesus."

The last meaningful words of Mom Voorheis's life were then spoken. With the same sense of closure that God gave to His creation on the sixth day, Mom simply said, "That's good." Reaching out her hand to touch the face of her son, Mom used that gesture to commend Eldon to the care of God with the assurance of answered prayer.

Turning from the casket, Mom Voorheis instantly lapsed back into the sightless and senseless world of her senility. Friends who gathered around her expecting recognition received only an involuntary smile and a gracious nod. As quickly as we could, Janet and I took Mom out the door, into the car, and back to the nursing home. No words passed between us, and when we left her bedside to go to the cemetery, her fatigue had already put her into deep sleep.

Mom Voorheis taught us a lesson in the funeral—one that can never be forgotten. We had assumed that her senility had robbed her of all her mental functions. Because she did not recognize us or respond to us on a conscious level, we concluded that the mom we knew no longer existed except in body, face, and memory. How wrong we were. The human brain is a mystery of countless cells that can store a lifetime of memories and a depth of functions beyond the reach of human probe. I now believe that somewhere in the unexplored realms of human thought there is a connector by which we communicate directly with God. Through the cultivation of prayer, the discipline of the Word, and the experiences of faith, we open communication lines with God that are premonitions of eternity. In fact, I also believe that our spiritual sensitivities sharpen as we grow old and especially when the conscious functions of thinking begin to dull through the natural processes of aging, the trauma of terminal illness, or the mysterious onset of senility.

Robert Fine served as senior pastor of the First Free Methodist Church at Seattle Pacific University in Seattle, Washington, for sixteen years. Cancer cut short his ministry in his middle fifties. When I visited him in the hospital a few days before his death, he moaned with pain as he tried to lift his head and greet me. Still, despite the yellowing of jaundice, his eyes gleamed as he said, "David, I'm so glad that I cultivated the life of the mind. As my body gets weaker, my mind seems stronger than ever. I can think and dream better than ever. Cancer can't take that away from me."

In Mom's case, we saw a momentary opening into the world of thought where she still lived. Sixty-three years as a faithful wife and forty-four years as a pastor's partner must have filled her hours with satisfying memories. Now, in that same world, only one thing mattered. She needed to know the answer to a half-century of daily prayers. Was her son saved? Beneath the confused world of her conscious mind, one can imagine the intensity of focus upon this one remaining question. If only Eldon's salvation was assured, Mom would be content at the center of her soul. From this perspective, we understand what happened in the funeral home that day. Her last prayer was answered, and her highest purpose in life was fulfilled.

Since witnessing Mom's moment when the curtain on revelation rose so fleetingly, I've learned about other children of Christian parents who have had similar experiences. Audrey Hostetter, wife of President D. Ray Hostetter at Messiah College, tells of her father's stroke, which left him "brain dead." After several hopeless months on a respirator, the doctor asked Audrey and her sister if they wanted to make a decision on whether or not to disconnect the life-support system. They prayed, talked, and wept their way to the soul-wrenching decision. Because the father whom they knew and loved no longer seemed to live, they tried to respect his wishes by asking the doctor to pull the plug. Entering their father's room for the last time to say good-bye, Audrey bent down close to her father's ear and whispered, "Daddy, now you can go home to be with Jesus." At the sound of her whisper, a teardrop appeared in the corner of her father's eye. For months he had not shown the slightest hint of a human response, and the monitor above his bed still showed the flat line of a dead brainstem. Yet at the mention of the name of Jesus, a teardrop revealed human understanding at a depth beyond the reach of the monitor. When Audrey reported the response to the doctor, he immediately reversed the decision. A teardrop had revealed a lively faith in a brain diagnosed as dead by the most sophisticated of human technology.

While still reflecting on the meaning of Audrey's story, I listened intently while Dr. Billy Melvin, executive director of the National Association of Evangelicals, told about the final hours of his aged mother. She lay on a bed at home in a coma. Dr. Melvin's brother slept in the next room so that he could listen to her breathing and check regularly on her condition. Throughout her life, Mrs. Melvin had been noted for her singing. Old age had taken the quality of her voice from her, and she had stopped singing solos in church years ago. Who then can explain what happened on the night she died? Dr. Melvin's brother awakened to the distant sound of a singing voice. Although he does not remember the song or its words, he has no doubt about the voice. His mother was singing with all of the brilliance of tone and timbre that he remembered hearing as a youth. Before he could get to her, however, the singing stopped, and when he bent down to hear her breathing, she was gone. Not a shred of doubt exists in the minds of Dr. Melvin or his brother. Their mother's singing marked the moment when she joined heaven's choir! In another unforgettable moment of revelation, an aged parent in a coma reminds us that spiritual sensitivities are sharpest in the presence of death.

Stephen's Vision

Are we dealing with fantasy, coincidence, or revelation? If we take seriously the Word of God, we know the answer. In the Acts of the Apostles, Stephen the deacon evoked the murderous wrath of the Sanhedrin by preaching Jesus Christ and Him crucified as the only hope for their salvation. Death was imminent as the Jewish leaders were cut to the heart by the truth and gnashed their teeth in hatred. "But Stephen, full of the Holy Spirit, looked up to heaven and saw the glory of God, and Jesus standing at the right hand of God. 'Look,' he said, 'I see heaven open and the Son of Man standing at the right hand of God' " (Acts 7:55-56).

Stephen's vision was too much for the Jewish leaders of the Sanhedrin. They covered their ears, yelled at the tops of their voices, rushed toward their victim, dragged him out of the city, and stoned him to death. Eyewitnesses attested to the event, including Saul of Tarsus, who later confronted the same Christ on the Damascus Road.

Why not believe in "Stephen's vision" today? Medical specialists now recognize what is called "the Lazarus effect" for persons who come back from the dead with visions of life beyond the grave. Equally real are the moments of revelation for aging Christian parents who may appear to be dead or at the door of death. As in Stephen's vision, their mind clears, heaven opens, and Christ is seen in the glorious fulfillment of His promise. Although the experience is not guaranteed for all Christian parents who are approaching death, we must not deny them this privilege or discount its reality. On the contrary, I expect that a collection of true stories from other children of Christian parents would settle any doubt about eternity and cause us to think twice before giving up on our parents in the last moments of life. "Stephen's vision" may be far more common than we think.

Celebrating Eternity

From "Stephen's vision" we learn to celebrate eternity. Earlier we established the principle that old age is an extension of the life that we have lived. Now, with the knowledge of "Stephen's vision," we realize that *eternity is also an extension of the life we have lived.* Enoch, in the Old Testament, is our model. In Genesis, we read Enoch's epitaph, "Enoch walked with God; then he was no more, because God took him away" (5:24). Like Enoch, the path that we walk in life will be the same path that we walk into eternity.

"Stephen's vision," therefore, is not an unnatural phenomenon. Rather, it is a window into the soul of the Christian and a preview of the glory of Christ. All of us have quoted the phrase, "As we live, we will die." Now we can add the corollary, "As we die, we will live."

Another lesson we learn from the "St. Stephen's vision" is *to be alert to the sharpened spiritual sensitivies of elderly parents as they approach death.* In my clinical training as a hospital chaplain, I was taught that any one of the five senses can be acutely sharpened as the body weakens. In fact, an elusive "sixth sense" may take over. I recall an occasion when the son of a dying father whispered some instructions into the ear of his sister in the far corner of the hospital room. None of us standing around the bed heard what he said. Their father, however, roused from his semicomatose state and repeated every word. Another time, a patient who had not been informed of her terminal condition picked up all of the cues of body language from her family and announced, "It's over, isn't it?"

We must not forget another side of the story. Dr. J. C. McPheeters, esteemed second president of Asbury Theological Seminary, suffered a debilitating stroke at the age of ninety-four. Until the stroke, he traveled for the seminary, preached in churches across the country, quoted Scripture by chapters, and worked out daily with barbells. The stroke, however, left him crippled and speechless. One of the saddest pictures in my memory is to see Dr. McPheeters sitting in the dining room of the rehabilitation center with a huge rubber bib covering his chest. I helped him put a spoonful of peas into the good side of his mouth. Then his eyes requested a drink of milk. I put the straw into the good side of his mouth and he took a strong sip of milk. When he did, milk and peas ran out from the sagging side and down on the bib.

Never would I rob Dr. McPheeters of his dignity. The story is told only to draw the contrast with the glory of a moment that followed. In the annual Wilmore Camp Meeting that summer, friends took Dr. McPheeters in a wheelchair to the Sunday morning service for what they knew to be the last time. Down in front of the tabernacle, Dr. McPheeters met Dr. E. A. Seamands, ninety-one, one of the great missionaries of the twentieth century. As a civil engineer, Dr. Seamands had complemented the evangelistic ministry of E. Stanley Jones in India by building over 175 churches in South India and earning the endearment of the Indian people by being known as "Tata" or "Grandfather" among them. When the two came together at camp meeting, they got into position for all the congregation to see and sang without hesitation every word of the beloved hymn,

> It is joy unspeakable and full of glory,
> Full of glory, full of glory.
> It is joy unspeakable and full of glory,
> Oh, the half has never yet been told.

From such experiences, we learn how to minister to our aging parents as their spiritual senses are honed in their final days. Even if they are in a coma, victims of advanced senility, or suffering excruciating pain, our ministry is to say a simple prayer, quote a familiar Scripture, or sing a favorite hymn. Whether or not they hear us and respond is unimportant. For them, and for us, a deeper work of the Holy Spirit may be taking place.

Still another lesson that we can learn from "Stephen's vision" is *not to give up too quickly on the life of our aging parents.* Contrary to common opinion, medicine is not an exact science. Physicians will be the first to admit their diagnoses cannot account for all of the factors that predict life or death. Certainly, they cannot diagnose the sharpening of spiritual sensitivities as death approaches. While none of us wants to suffer without mercy, perhaps the apostle Paul was right when he thanked God for the privilege of suffering as one of the ways that drew him closer to Christ.

Living wills, in which we state our wishes for the doctor and our family if we are terminally ill and incompetent, are fast becoming standard instruments for life-and-death decisions. In fact, Congress has passed a law requiring that hospitals receiving federal funds provide counseling on the options available to patients in the event of incompetency due to illness. While recognizing the merits of living wills and hospital counseling on these matters, we dare not cheapen life or speed death. Christians must sound the alarm when a suicide handbook entitled *Final Exit* is a national best-seller, and Dr. Jack Kevorkian assists the terminally ill in dying. The sanctity and dignity of life from beginning to end must be held with biblical conviction. To assume that euthanasia is morally different from abortion because one involves conscious choice while the other involves an innocent victim is to ignore the fundamental fact that life itself is a divine gift, which we cannot devalue or destroy without sinning against God. So, as our parents age and need us to help make life-and-death decisions, the evidence of "Stephen's vision" prompts us to err on the side of life.

Finally, "Stephen's vision" confirms for us *the reality of heaven*. If we are honest, each of us has uncertainties about heaven because our human nature cannot fully comprehend its spiritual nature. As fully as we believe the Word of God and anticipate being in the presence of Christ, our humanity reminds us that we have no eyewitnesses who have been to heaven and back. Perhaps we are wrong. If we listen and learn from our aging Christian parents, we will see all of the reality of heaven that we need.

CHAPTER 13

Learning from Jesus
Caregiving

How does God's commandment "Honor your father and mother" apply to aging parents in changing times? How did Jesus fulfill the spirit of this commandment as an example for us?

Does Jesus understand what it means for us to care for aging parents in contemporary circumstances? In Jesus' time people lived only half as long as we do today. He knew nothing about Medicare payments, medical breakthroughs, nursing homes, and living wills. Yet, for those of us who believe in the timeless truth of God's Word, Jesus understands every dilemma we face, every decision we make, every pain we suffer, and every doubt we hold in caring for our aging parents. If we demand specifics for every situation, we will be disappointed. But if we build on biblical principles, Jesus will teach us the full meaning of filial honor—a commandment of the law, which He taught as infallible truth and a concept of the Spirit, which He lived as a flawless example.

When the rich young man asked Jesus which commandments to obey in order to gain eternal life, the Master chose "Honor your father and mother" among the six which He highlighted. To Him, filial honor went beyond a commandment to be obeyed; it was a spirit to be lived. His example backs up His teaching. In the moments when Jesus' relationship with His parents puts His teaching to the test, He personalizes the principles we need to guide us today. Thus filial honor becomes another proof that the Word of God is timeless and that Jesus Christ is our best friend.

The Principle of Filial Obedience

As the base upon which long-term relationships with our parents are built, Jesus teaches us the meaning of filial honor through His obedience to His parents. Go back in your mind to the familiar episode when Jesus, the twelve-year-old boy, missed the caravan and stayed behind in the temple to ask and answer questions of the priests and scholars. When His parents missed him after three days' journey and returned to Jerusalem to find Him, His mother vented her frustration in the question, "Son, why have you treated us like this? Your father and I have been anxiously searching for you" (Luke 2:48).

Revealing His adolescent humanity, Jesus spouted, "Why were you searching for me? . . . Didn't you know I had to be in my Father's house?" (Luke 2:49).

In turn, Joseph and Mary responded like typical parents of a teenager: "They did not understand what he was saying to them" (Luke 2:50). But after that early show of independence with its prediction of things to come, Jesus then "went down to Nazareth with them and was obedient to them" (Luke 2:51).

Filial honor begins with filial obedience. A disrespectful child will not become a respectful caregiver when parents grow old. One of the most frightening facts coming out of studies of domestic violence in families is to find that abuse breeds abuse from generation to generation. Children who learn violence in the home of their parents practice violence in their own homes with their own children. Escalating evidence of "elderly abuse" in our society should make us pause.

Children who do not obey parents in early age may benignly neglect and physically abuse them in old age. But given this reality, can we not also conclude that the honor of obedience in early age becomes the honor of care in old age? Filial obedience pays its benefit in the quality of care that adult children give to their aging parents just at the time when they are most needy.

According to Luke's Gospel, filial obedience has another benefit for both children and parents that bears directly upon their relationship in old age. Jesus' obedience to His parents provided the discipline within which He "grew in wisdom and stature, and in favor with God and men" (Luke 2:52). Physical, psychological, social, and spiritual growth all converge in this short verse. Working together along the natural lines of human development, they become beautifully tuned and balanced in a model of maturity that is confirmed in Jesus' adulthood.

Any one of us who has cared for aging parents knows that every part of our personality is put to the test of maturity in times of crisis. Physically, our energies are drained; psychologically, our nerves are frayed; socially, our relationships are strained; and spiritually, our faith is challenged. To honor our aging parents under these conditions requires the recognition that our obedience and their discipline helped prepare us for caring in crisis. Filial obedience lends credence to the adage, "Whatever goes around comes around." In the cycle of the generations, filial obedience in early age becomes personal maturity in adulthood and filial care in old age. One cannot be separated from the other. Following in their turn, filial obedience, personal maturity, and filial care give meaning to the beginning, middle, and end of the sixth commandment, "Honor your father and mother."

The Principle of Filial Responsibility

In Mark 6:3 we are given a description of Jesus' family as He returned home for His first visit after opening His public ministry. Jesus had left Nazareth as a common carpenter; He returned as a master teacher.

Neighbors who knew Him could not believe that transformation. Skeptically, they raised the question, "Isn't this Mary's son and the brother of James, Joseph, Judas, and Simon? Aren't His sisters here with us?"

Three facts immediately come to our attention. First, we learn again that Jesus is the firstborn and eldest son of Joseph and Mary. Second, Jesus came from a large family, including four brothers and an unknown number of sisters. Third, the absence of Joseph's name heading the family roster suggests that he had died and left Mary a widow. If so, responsibility for Mary and the family fell to Jesus. We already know that He did not leave home to begin his public ministry until the "coming out" age of thirty-one, according to Jewish tradition. We also need to realize that during the silent years between the age of twelve in the temple and the age of thirty-one when He appeared on the banks of the Jordan, Jesus made the transition from filial obedience to filial responsibility. Especially if His mother was widowed, Jesus had to assume the father's role for the family—earning a living, consoling His mother, and nurturing His younger brothers and sisters. Knowing Jesus' integrity as we do, no stretch of the imagination is needed to conclude that He accepted the father's role and assumed the filial responsibility that fell to Him. With that same assurance of integrity, we can also conclude that He did not leave home until the care of His mother and the livelihood of His family had been assured. Although His townsfolk ridiculed the idea that the carpenter had become a rabbi, they did not give the slightest hint that He might have neglected His family by leaving home. One can envision Jesus leaving a debt-free family home, a stable carpentry business with the brothers as partners, domestic help from the sisters, and an extended family of aunts and uncles, nieces and nephews, grandsons and granddaughters—all serving as the support base for His mother, Mary.

Although pension funds, medical insurance, and nursing homes give assurance to our aging parents today, they lack the personalized value of filial responsibility in Jesus' time. From His example, we need to learn that economic provision is only part of our filial responsibility. Aging parents fear isolation and abandonment as much as if not more than sickness and poverty. Our filial responsibility calls for us to pay close attention to the relational support system we provide for our aging parents, especially during the times of transition when physical relocation is required. It takes time for a new place and new people to become "home" for our aging parents, but with interim support from the immediate family, the transition can be amazing. My sister's eighty-seven-year-old mother-in-law, for instance, fought the sale of the family home and the move into a retirement center. Now she is equally adamant about leaving the retirement center in Detroit, Michigan, to live with her daughter in a new home in Sun City, Nevada. She will miss her friends, social hours, worship services, and most of all, the opportunity to take classes in Spanish and accounting, which she could not take as an immigrant daughter from Armenia without the privilege of high school. Still, the move must eventually be made. When it happens, she will need her son, her daughter, and my sister, her daughter-in-law, to give her full support at an age when a transcontinental move, even to be with her own family, is like a trip to the moon. As Jesus taught us about these moments, filial responsibility will be the signal of filial honor.

The Principle of Filial Independence

At times, Jesus' response to His mother and family seems to contradict His sensitivity for filial responsibility. When someone announced that His mother, brothers, and sisters appeared in the crowd and wanted to speak to Him, Jesus spoke a conundrum:

> "Who is my mother, and who are my brothers?" Pointing to his disciples, he said, "Here are my mother and my brothers. For whoever does the will of my Father in heaven is my brother and sister and mother." *Matthew 12:48-50*

Even more confusing is Jesus' earlier response in His exhortation to the disciples before sending them out to preach, teach, and heal:

> Anyone who loves his father or mother more than me is not worthy of me; anyone who loves his son or daughter more than me is not worthy of me; and anyone who does not take his cross and follow me is not worthy of me. *Matthew 10:37-38*

Take the force of this hard saying one more step. Luke heard the same exhortation, but with different meaning. He recalls Jesus saying,

> If anyone comes to me and does not hate his father and mother, his wife and children, his brothers and sisters—yes, even his own life—he cannot be my disciple. *Luke 14:26*

Was Jesus contradicting His own commandment, "Honor your father and mother?" Or was He establishing the principle of filial independence that sets children free to be themselves and put Christ first in their lives? I contend for the latter position. In the natural course of human development, filial dependence must give way to filial independence. Otherwise, our growth as persons is stunted and our first loyalty to God cannot be given.

As much as it may hurt, I have always advocated a love that lets go of our children, our protégés, and our converts. The saddest sight I know is to see children who have never established their own identity. I even wonder at sons and daughters who forsake marriage or career opportunities in order to care for their parents. For some, this may be their ministry. For others, it may be a flight from independence. I must confess that my ego took a blow when students at Seattle Pacific University never connected "David L. McKenna Hall" with our oldest son, Douglas, a professor of business who teaches classes in the building—or with our youngest son, Robert, who took his B.A. and M.B.A. classes in the hall named after his father. Yet I must learn that my sons need to be free of my identity in order to become the persons God calls them to be and to follow Him wherever He may lead.

Every son and daughter must make a declaration of independence from his or her parents. The declaration may have to be as forceful as choosing between parents and family, parents and career, parents and vocation, or parents and faith. In our case, we had to leave aging parents in Michigan to the care of a brother and sister in order to follow the call of God to the presidency of a Christian university in Seattle, Washington. Others may not have to answer such a distant call, but all of us must declare our filial independence if we are to grow to our potential as individuals created in the image of God.

Filial independence is even more important to our spiritual individuality. When Jesus talked about hating our spouse and children, parents and siblings in order to be worthy of Him, He did not condone a sinful emotion. Rather, He established the principle of filial independence on spiritual grounds. His radical call to self-sacrifice included the decision to choose between two of our greatest and sometimes competing loves—our God and our family. To choose God may appear to be hatred for family, but this is not so. It is the choice between competing loves in which God must be first. But when this choice is made, the family does not suffer. In my own case, when I chose to answer the call of God in transcontinental moves from Michigan to the state of Washington, and then later from Washington to Kentucky, the changes could have been disastrous for our junior and senior-high children. But when I began to second-guess the will of God during the tough moments of transition, He invariably pointed to the positive impact on our children as confirming evidence of His call. Does not the same principle hold for our relationship with our parents? We honor our father and mother when we declare filial independence as Jesus did. Without a clean, clear break, the carpenter could never become the rabbi, and the Son of Man could never have fulfilled His mission as the Son of God.

The Principle of Filial Stewardship

As we might expect, Jesus does not forget our financial responsibility
to our parents as another way of spelling out the commandment
"Honor your father and mother." In a complex passage of Scripture
dealing with a technicality of the Mosaic law, Jesus tells the Pharisees
and some teachers of the law,

> You have a fine way of setting aside the commands of God in
> order to observe your own traditions! For Moses said, "Honor
> your father and mother," and, "Anyone who curses his father
> or mother must be put to death." But you say that if a man says
> to his father or mother: "Whatever help you might otherwise
> have received from me is Corban" (that is, a gift devoted to
> God), then you no longer let him do anything for his father or
> mother. Thus you nullify the word of God by your tradition
> that you have handed down. And you do many things like that.
> *Mark 7:9-13*

Jesus' purpose in this passage is to condemn the Pharisees and
scribes for inventing religious regulations that become more important than responding to human need. *Corban* is the key word. It means
a gift of money or property that is laid upon the altar of God and set
apart exclusively for sacred use. Certainly such an act is intrinsically
good and expressly spiritual. Setting aside our resources solely for
sacred purposes is not unlike dedicating ourselves wholly for God's
use. By sanctifying our resources we sanctify ourselves. The Pharisees, however, had twisted the meaning of *Corban* to avoid meeting
their personal debts and their filial responsibilities. A debtor, for
instance, could declare the amount of his debt as *Corban* so that his
creditor could make no claim upon the money. By this concoction,
Corban became a spiritualized "Chapter 11" to declare bankruptcy
and escape creditors.

Corban had taken on another twisted meaning to which Jesus alludes. In a fit of anger, a son or daughter could pronounce *Corban* upon their parents as a curse to avoid further communication with them or responsibility for them. In this case, a twist of the law becomes a perversion of the law. *Corban,* originally a sacred concept, is now used to justify a curse in direct violation of the Mosaic law. Instead of the son or daughter's curse being a reason for death by execution, which the law originally required, it is now extolled by the Pharisees as a spiritual virtue.

Jesus' choice of the commandment "Honor your father and mother" in refuting the pharisaical interpretation of *Corban* is not incidental. He cites instances in which a child pronounces *Corban* upon a gift of money and then refuses to help his parents in need. While the Pharisees spiritualized such an act, Jesus denounced it as the sin of using tradition to break the law. To Him, the commandment took precedence over tradition and human need took precedence over a "spiritualized" interpretation. To neglect needy parents under the guise of spiritual priority is a sin for which Jesus had no patience. We can be sure, then, that He did not embark upon His spiritual mission without adequate financial provision for His mother and family. Otherwise His words would have come back to haunt Him. Following His example, we too will recognize the priority of our parents in providing for their financial needs. The principle of filial stewardship teaches us that we cannot justify neglecting our parents, even on spiritual grounds, and still please God.

The Principle of Filial Care

After declaring His independence, Jesus did not forget His mother. In the midst of His suffering on the cross, He still thought about her rather than Himself. Looking down upon the scene of wailing women, Jesus realized that His mother suffered most. So, speaking directly to Mary and John, He bonded His beloved mother with His beloved disciple: "Dear woman, here is your son," and to the disciple, "Here is your mother" (John 19:26-27).

John, the disciple to whom Jesus refers and the author of the Gospel, then adds the autobiographical footnote, "From that time on, this disciple took her into his home" (John 19:27).

No moment is more tender or touching in all of Scripture. When Jesus knew He could no longer fulfill His obligation as a son, He made an alternative provision for the care of His mother. Not unlike our contemporary circumstances in which alternatives to personalized care of aging parents are often required, Jesus asked John to take His place and become Mary's surrogate son.

What happened to Jesus' brother and sisters, we might ask? I suspect that their care continued for her physical and social needs, but only John could become her spiritual son with whom she could share all that she "treasured . . . in her heart" (Luke 2:51). Who better could feel the grief in those numbing hours after the Crucifixion? Despite her unfailing faith, Mary must have feared that her Son had died without fulfilling the messianic promise that she had been given. Not until the angel at the empty tomb gave her word of Christ's resurrection would Mary's grief be broken. During those critical hours after the Crucifixion and into the years ahead when only faith could foresee the redemptive outcome of Jesus' death, John would be her son.

Alternative care for aging parents is a grim reality in our fast-moving, urban world. For all intents and purposes, the extended family is extinct and "in-law" apartments are too costly to consider. More and more, alternative care is the most viable option. In some instances, we may have the resources to provide housekeeping services for our parents or pay someone to live with them. Even then, the time will probably come when a decision about a total life-care facility looms large. We will not escape the guilt of that decision. Most of us, at one time or another, have felt as if we would have our parents live with us rather than in a nursing home. But when the moment of crisis arrives, reality checks in. Whether it is the size of our home, the mobility of our career, the priority of our growing children, the clash of our personalities, or the limits of our finances, we will be like Jim, Beth, Bob, and Bonnie at the beginning of this book. Alternative care is the option, but what kind of care will it be?

Jesus shows us that a lifetime of filial love is the bond that holds our aging parents through the temporary crises and permanent adjustments of aging. The kind of alternative care is secondary to the assurance of filial love. By being caregivers first and caretakers second, we will be following the model and reflecting the spirit of Jesus in giving filial care to our parents as He did to His mother.

Return to the question, "Does Jesus understand what it means for us to care for our aging parents in contemporary circumstances?" The answer is unequivocally yes even though He never had to deal with such modern inventions as nursing homes and Medicare. Instead of dealing with the specifics of changing systems, He personalizes for us the principles of filial honor to fulfill in letter and spirit the meaning of the fifth commandment, "Honor your father and mother." Following His example, our role as caregivers for aging parents is clear. We are to:

- Require *filial obedience* in each generation so that our children will mature as persons capable of being caregivers for aging parents.
- Accept *filial responsibility* for the care of our aging parents according to our position, resources, and role in the family.
- Declare the *filial independence* from our parents when needed to reach our potential as persons and give God first loyalty.
- Exercise *filial stewardship* to provide for the financial needs of our aging parents as a spiritual priority.

- Assure *filial care* on a short and long-term basis for aging parents with an emphasis upon relational and spiritual support.

Need we say more? Sooner or later your phone will ring, and you will come to the moment when your parents need you most. By following the principles of loving care that Jesus taught us, you will honor your parents and please your God, even in these changing times.

Rights and Responsibilities of the Christian Caregiver

I Have a Right:

1. To take care of myself

2. To seek help from others even though my relative may object. I recognize the limits of my endurance

3. To maintain facets of my own life that do not include the person I care for

4. To get angry, be depressed, and express other difficult feelings

5. To reject any attempt by my relative (either conscious or unconscious) to manipulate me

6. To take pride in what I am accomplishing and to applaud the courage it has sometimes taken

I Have a Responsibility:

1. To assume my share of the care for my aging parents

2. To listen to the concerns of my aging parents and explain, as best I can, the reasons for my decisions

3. To maintain, whenever possible, the facets of my aging parents' life that give them independence and dignity

4. To create a climate of joy and hope for my aging parents

5. To seek to understand why my aging parents resort to manipulation

6. To take pride in the continuing accomplishments of my aging parents and applaud their courage for small wins

7. To protect my individuality and my right to make a life for myself

7. To recognize that the gift of self-sacrifice, which my aging parents once gave to me, is now mine to give in return

Endnotes

Chapter 1

1. Tim Stafford, *As Our Years Increase* (New York: Harper Paperbacks, 1991), 6.
2. Ibid., 21.
3. Francine and Robert Moskowitz, *Parenting Your Aging Parents* (Woodland Hills, Calif.: Key Publications, 1991), 2-3.
4. *Seattle Post-Intelligencer,* November 27, 1991.

Chapter 2

1. Robert N. Bellah, et al., *Habits of the Heart: Individualism and Commitment in American Life* (New York: Harper & Row, 1985).

Chapter 3

1. Paul Rees, "I Shall Go to My Grave," *The Asbury Herald* (Fall 1991), Asbury Theological Seminary, Wilmore, Kentucky.
2. Elton Trueblood, *While It Is Day: An Autobiography* (New York: Harper & Row, 1974).

Chapter 7

1. Delbert E. McHenry, "Expectations and Relocation Stress of the Elderly, (unpublished research), Seattle Pacific University, Seattle, Washington, 1979.

Chapter 9

1. Robert Wuthnow, *Acts of Compassion* (Princeton, N.J.: Princeton University Press, 1991).

CPSIA information can be obtained at www.ICGtesting.com
Printed in the USA
LVOW10s0252251013

358560LV00006B/33/P